HUMAN LIFE STYLING

*the text of this book is printed
on 100% recycled paper*

Also by James Presley

Public Defender
   (*in collaboration with Gerald W. Getty*)

Vitamin B_6: The Doctor's Report
   (*in collaboration with John M. Ellis, M.D.*)

"Please, Doctor, Do Something!"
   (*in collaboration with Joe D. Nichols, M.D.*)

Center of the Storm: Memoirs of John T. Scopes
   (*in collaboration with John T. Scopes*)

HUMAN
LIFE
STYLING

KEEPING WHOLE IN THE TWENTIETH CENTURY

John C. McCamy, M.D., and James Presley

HARPER COLOPHON BOOKS

HARPER & ROW, PUBLISHERS

NEW YORK, HAGERSTOWN, SAN FRANCISCO, LONDON

A hardcover edition of this book is published by Harper & Row, Publishers, Inc.

HUMAN LIFE STYLING. Copyright © 1975 by John C. McCamy, M.D., and James Presley. All rights reserved. Printed in the United States of America. No part of this book may be used or reproduced in any manner whatsoever without written permission except in the case of brief quotations embodied in critical articles and reviews. For information address Harper & Row, Publishers, Inc., 10 East 53d Street, New York, N.Y. 10022. Published simultaneously in Canada by Fitzhenry & Whiteside Limited, Toronto.

Designed by Sidney Feinberg

First HARPER COLOPHON edition published 1977

ISBN: 0-06-090540-9

81 10 9 8 7 6 5

We are grateful to the following for permission to reproduce copyrighted material in this book:

The figures in Chapter 3 are from *Replenish the Earth* by G. Tyler Miller, Jr. Copyright © 1972 by Wadsworth Publishing Company, Inc., Belmont, Calif. Reprinted by permission of the publisher.

Material relating to the Club of Rome is from *The Limits to Growth* by Donella H. Meadows, Dennis L. Meadows, Jorgen Randers, William Behrens, III. A Potomac Associates book published by Universe Books, New York. Copyright © 1972 by Dennis L. Meadows.

The chart on carbohydrate metabolism in Chapter 4 is from *Nutrition in Preventive Dentistry: Science and Practice* by Abraham E. Nizel, D.M.D., M.S.D., F.A.C.D. Copyright © 1972 by W. B. Saunders Co., Philadelphia. Reprinted by permission of the publisher and the author.

The photographs of Maori people in Chapter 4, are from *Nutrition and Physical Degeneration* by Weston A. Price, D.D.S. Copyright © 1970 by the Price-Pottenger Foundation. Reprinted through the courtesy of the Price-Pottenger Foundation, Inc., Santa Monica, Calif.

The exercise programs in Chapter 5 are from *The New Aerobics* by Kenneth H. Cooper, M.D., M.P.H. Copyright © 1970 by Kenneth H. Cooper. Reprinted by permission of the publisher, M. Evans and Company, New York.

To the Living Past:

> Philip Kapleau, Roshi
> Emanuel Cheraskin, M.D., D.M.D.
> And their lineage

The Future:

> To Monica McCamy and her five billion brothers and sisters who will learn they can choose their own destinies

The Now:

> To the highest in me, and the highest in you, the reader, who will recognize that we can choose now to be whole.
> —JOHN C. McCAMY

For these four, especially:

> My wife, Fran Presley
> Our children, John Presley and Ann Presley
> My agent and friend, Blanche Gregory
> —JAMES PRESLEY

Contents

Acknowledgments   xi

1. The Concept of Human Life Styling   1

2. The Four Horsemen of Health   17

3. Ecological You   41

4. Nutrition—Keeping It Simple   57

5. Descendants of Hunters   94

6. How to Relax and Reduce Stress   120

7. Does It Work?/Case Histories   140

8. To Renew a Nation   158

Appendix I: A Directory of Prevention-Oriented Organizations   169

Appendix II: Seven-Day Health Diary   172

An Essay on Sources   175

An Armamentarium of Healthful Reading   187

Acknowledgments

Although I never knew him personally, my lineage as a doctor in preventive medicine traces at least as far as Weston A. Price, D.D.S., whose monumental, classic work on nutrition and degeneration is one of the great books that have stimulated so many others in this country. W. D. Currier, M.D., studied his work and developed much of his approach to medicine from it, as did Melvin E. Page, D.D.S., who developed a holistic approach and was one of the founders of the Southern Academy of Clinical Nutrition.

My fellow members in the Southern Academy of Clinical Nutrition have taught me much and I would like to single them out for credit for much of the material in this book. It was my privilege to participate in a seven-year study in preventive medicine under the auspices of the academy, the results of which Emanuel Cheraskin, M.D., D.M.D., and associates published in a number of articles.

Dr. Cheraskin's elegant, clear approach to true health states, most of all, has shown me a path through the maze of health data. He and W. Marshall Ringsdorf, Jr., are the founders of predictive medicine; his concepts provided the framework for the practical application of Human Life Styling.

It was also my privilege to work briefly with Dr. Kenneth H. Cooper and observe his work at the Aerobics Institute in Dallas, Texas.

So many have inspired me by their contact and examples: Hans Selye, M.D., Linus Pauling, Ph.D., Roger Williams, Ph.D., Adelle Davis, Joe D. Nichols, M.D., John M. Ellis, M.D., Ida Rolf, Ph.D., Rill Williams, Ph.D., Melvin Gardner, M.D., and F. Boland McCamy, D.D.S., my brother.

I wish to acknowledge my appreciation for my parents, Roy and Lucy McCamy, who reared me with great dedication.

Everybody in the Association of Humanistic Psychology has played some part in guiding me. The Esalen spirit has been a continuing influence and inspiration.

I owe a special debt to Roshi Philip Kapleau, my Zen teacher, who has taught me the path of self-development. Through meditation training he has helped me to see my true mission. And I am grateful for my hatha-yoga teachers, who have helped prepare me.

JOHN C. McCAMY, M.D.

I wish to acknowledge personally my wife, Fran Presley, a major source of encouragement in the writing of this book, for her incisive editorial suggestions; Ruth Pollack, our editor at Harper & Row; Blanche C. Gregory, my agent and highly valued friend; Corbett Anderson, for his chart work; F. L. Walraven, for photographic reproductions; and Elizabeth Wright, who gave up a vacation trip in order to type the final manuscript.

JAMES PRESLEY

HUMAN LIFE STYLING

1

The Concept of Human Life Styling

College student Larry Malone and his three friends were healthy, energetic and vigorous. Their doctor had pronounced them so. This made them perfect subjects for an experiment.

The physician-author of this book (Dr. John C. McCamy) and several medical colleagues wanted to find out what would happen if a healthy person went to a doctor and asked for health care. We suggested that Larry and his friends present themselves to the health center of their university.

They did. Larry explained that they were completely well and had no complaints. However, since this was a "health" center, they wanted advice on how to *stay* well.

Larry was first taken behind a curtain. There, a doctor told him in sympathetic and confidential tones, "It's all right. Our records are private. You can just tell me about your disease. No one else will know."

"But I don't have a disease," said Larry. "I'm well."

"Yes, I know," reassured the doctor. "We won't tell your parents, the dean or anybody else. We'll give you a shot of penicillin—"

"I don't have a venereal disease," persisted Larry, "or anything else."

Larry was not treated for venereal disease, nor were he and his friends told how to stay well, but he *was* referred to a psychiatrist. If he did not have a physical disease, then he obviously had a mental disorder.

A psychologist had given us the idea for this experiment, and he had predicted the results accurately. The idea of a *healthy* person going to a doctor or a clinic is unheard of in traditional medicine. A conventionally oriented doctor would be mildly astonished if he were visited by a patient who considered himself to be without symptoms. He probably would tell him to go home and try to stay healthy. Both his training and his practice have revolved around the treatment of disease, not its prevention.

What could the doctor have told Larry Malone?

Quite a lot. Already there is a sufficient body of data that would enable one to predict which diseases Larry is likely to come down with, and die of, in the decades ahead. At age twenty Larry was doing the sensible thing. If he could find out which risks lay ahead in the dangerous years, he would be able to avoid them. He could change his health habits. By learning how to change his life style at an early age, he could become one of the positive statistics of medicine.

This book is about your life style.

Your life style is you. You are what you eat, drink, breathe, think and do. Therefore, what you become tomorrow depends upon what you do today. You are the only person in the world who can do what is necessary to make you healthy and happy.

Making your life style a healthy one involves the relatively new field of preventive medicine. As the Larry Malone anecdote illustrated, traditional medicine has always been oriented toward disease *treatment* and injury repair. This is what doctors are trained to do and it is what patients have come to expect of them. Thus, medicine as we know it today is concerned with disease diagnosis and treatment at the clinical level. Clinical diseases are those that have finally changed the body. In most cases, this means the last step in decades of degeneration. At best, an annual checkup will lead to an early diagnosis, which can be treated before the disease grows worse. It does not lead to prevention. A Canadian study, in fact, has indicated that you are just as well off to skip the annual physical examination and wait until symptoms occur before going to the doctor. And this is because medicine is almost totally devoted to disease treatment.

Think back to your own last visit to the doctor's office. Why did you go? What did he do? What was the result? Were you advised as to what you could do to achieve optimal health and how to maintain it? Or did he patch you up with a prescription and perhaps recommend surgery? The chances are that he performed some repair work, or checked you over, found nothing clinically wrong and told you that you were "all right." Yet you still felt bad. Your doctor was not to blame. He was doing what he was trained to do—what you expected him to do—and he probably did it well.

But it wasn't health care. True health care aims at prevention of future diseases, not their treatment after they've finally developed. A patient who goes to the doctor when he feels good could learn how to keep feeling good for the rest of his life. Every major degenerative disease is fully predictable and preventable in its first decade of development. We already have the necessary research data on the precipitating factors. These can be evaluated in any doctor's office, and this book will show you how you can evaluate some of these factors for yourself.

This concept of changing your life style in order to attain the optimal level of health is what we call Human Life Styling. It is a total health guidance system that grew out of the medical practice of the physician-author of this collaboration, Dr. John C. McCamy. At one time his practice consisted totally of disease treatment and injury repair. But as his patients kept returning to be patched up, he began to wonder why they suffered so much sickness.

He began investigating his patients' health habits. Many of them were repeatedly suffering from colds and strep throats in the warmer months of the year. Colds in the summer in sunny Florida! It didn't make sense. He questioned each afflicted patient in great detail. What did he drink? What did he eat? What else did he do? Without realizing it at the time, he was delving into their life styles.

On the basis of their answers, a pattern became noticeable. All the strep throat/cold patients consumed iced drinks and ate ices and sweets. Had these factors caused the colds in some way? It seemed plausible. The patients were instructed to stop eating sweets and to drink only liquids that were warm or at room temperature.

Respiratory infections almost completely disappeared in these patients. With a few other changes in life style, such as taking vitamin C daily, cold frequency dropped to zero.

Following this success, natural treatments were designed for a number of other illnesses. Patients with cystitis, or bladder inflammation, avoided coffee and drank fluids generously. Those with chronic lung disease took deep breaths, drank a lot of warm fluids, consumed large doses of vitamin C and refrained from smoking. For each disease there was a long, elaborate list of what to do and what not to do.

As he compiled his lists for the various illnesses, Dr. McCamy was amazed to discover that the same factors were involved in most illnesses. The pattern indicated that if a person attended to the dos and don'ts on the lists, he or she would prevent all those diseases!

A serious problem was that even after the lists were consolidated, there were still about forty things a person would have to do every day. Too many; it was hard for most patients to remember them all, much less carry them through. However, there were a few major areas in which a person could concentrate in order to prevent nearly all illness. Starting with this, Dr. McCamy began to boil down everything he knew about disease prevention into one simple, streamlined, practical system.

At about the same time he sought to meet as many leaders of preventive medicine as he could. He came into contact with persons such as Dr. Emanuel Cheraskin, Dr. Linus Pauling, Adelle Davis, Dr. Hans Selye, Dr. Melvin Page and other distinguished figures in the health field. He began to get in touch personally with people living a truly natural life. He spent a year practicing meditation, getting to know himself more intimately.

Out of these years grew the concept of Human Life Styling, a synthesis of what is natural for a truly normal person at this stage of evolution in the twentieth century.

But would it work?

He divided his patients into two groups. With five hundred of them he practiced disease treatment as usual, continuing to minister to them with the best techniques and drugs modern medicine had to offer. Meanwhile, another five hundred were introduced to the specific health advice in the Human Life Styling program.

The results: *Everyone* in the second group did better. Patients who followed the entire program demonstrated a 95 percent reduction in all symptoms, documented by annual rechecks and computer-graded questionnaires. This convinced Dr. McCamy and, extending the program to all his patients, he began to specialize in preventive medicine almost entirely.

The preventive features of Human Life Styling are based on the concept that disease is preventable. Predictive medicine, the contribution of Drs. Emanuel Cheraskin and W. Marshall Ringsdorf, Jr., of the University of Alabama Medical Center in Birmingham, strives to "*foretell* illness before it erupts in its classical form." Forewarned is fore-armed. With knowledge you can keep it from happening.

Predictability of diseases is based upon correlation studies. Such studies concern the various factors that appear consistently in patients with a specific disease. Cigarette smoking, for instance, is a leading correlation factor in the incidence of lung cancer. By stopping smoking or by having been a nonsmoker all along, you spectacularly lower your chances of getting lung cancer. Correlation studies single out such elements in the patients' life styles that probably contributed to the disease in the first place.

Doctors, then, can use the studies to predict the odds for a particular individual's getting a particular disease. Knowing what he is doing wrong, the patient can change the deleterious elements in his life style and thereby improve his odds on becoming ill and dying from that specific clinical disease.

This leads to the basic principle of Human Life Styling:

Disease is predictable. Disease is preventable.

Although the usefulness of preventive medicine may seem obvious to most people, the urgent need for it today may not be so apparent to many others. In this country we are obsessed with our deteriorating health, but we are not always aware of where we stand, both personally and nationally; degeneration, after all, is so gradual a process that it is difficult to keep sight of the overall pattern.

There are solid, unassailable reasons why we must turn to prevention as a way of life and health-care delivery. For one, the incidence of chronic diseases is rapidly increasing. A Department of Health, Education and Welfare report has demonstrated that the life expectancy for males in this country *dropped* during the decade from 1960 to 1970! Remember the startling revelations a few years ago on the autopsies performed on eighteen-year-old soldiers in Korea? Fifty percent already had coronary artery disease, representing a far-advanced stage. These were "apparently healthy young men." We are not only getting sicker in this country; we are also getting sicker younger. Our children are getting sicker. We are seeing bleeding ulcers in ten-year-old children. Ten years ago this rarely happened. In one study of subjects from ages seventeen to twenty-four, almost 50 percent had some form of degenerative disease.

It is an intolerable situation.

There are also urgent economic reasons for a greater emphasis on predictive and preventive medicine. The cost of hospital beds is climbing annually. It is now about $50 per day. Counting drugs and all services, one day in a coronary care unit can cost $200. Within a few years, according to an estimate reached by a medical magazine, coronary care will be as high as $1,000 per day. This would mean that if you have a coronary, you'll have to take $30,000 along with you to the hospital. And the demand for medical services continues to skyrocket.

The economic implications of preventive medicine are too strong to be ignored. In 1929, the total expenditure for medical care in this country was $3.5 billion. By 1972 it had reached $82 billion and was rising fantastically—far, far faster than the population. We have plunged into absurdity. We must start preventing our chronic diseases.

We hope that Human Life Styling will become an instrument to help achieve this goal.

As you undertake your own preventive program, as outlined in this book, it will be helpful to bear in mind three especially significant keys to the success of Human Life Styling. If you forget them, we suggest that you refer back to this chapter to refresh your memory.

1. *There is a difference between normal and average.* In medicine, we have tended to accept the terms "normal" and "average" as synonymous. If the average person is perfectly healthy, there could be no disagreement with this. A normal person should be healthy. But because of the rising tide of disease and degeneration in this country, we have installed the *relatively* healthy person as the average.

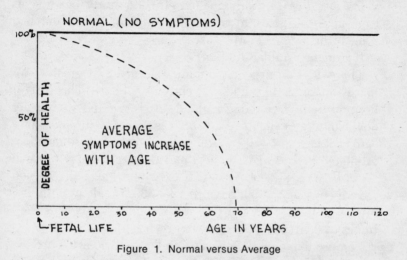

Figure 1. Normal versus Average

The so-called normal ranges in medicine have been compiled by studying a large group of people, approximately a thousand, most of whom are presumed to be healthy. The average readings on these, whether it is of their blood sugar or other laboratory data, blood pressure or cholesterol, are then presumed to be "normal." There may be a wide range of health conditions in that group. Some may be desperately ill. Some may feel fine. Some may be in perfect health, others may be at various points between there and near-death. Thus, all kinds of people help to establish the "norm," which necessarily is no more than an average.

Let's say that your cholesterol reading in your last blood test was 280 milligrams percent. Your doctor said it was in the "normal" range and you're okay. In many labs the "normal" ranges up to 310 milligrams. But if you accept that as normal, you must also accept as normal the fact that you are an odds-on favorite to have a heart attack within ten years.

What has taken the meaning out of the word "normal" as currently used is that the average patient now has many more symptoms than a decade ago; three times the number of complaints he had just ten years ago, in some studies. This indicates that our "normal" values will continue to shift because the average leans toward a less healthy population.

In this book we will be using the word "normal" as a synonym for "healthy"—a normal person is healthy in body and mind. We do not believe that a truly normal person should have any physical or mental complaints. He should feel good all the time. He should wake up feeling good and go to bed feeling good, with a happy, productive day in between.

In his laboratory tests the normal person generally will be within a very narrow range of values, rather than the wide ones that are accepted as normal in most tests. For instance, his cholesterol should be within 180 to 200, even though higher ranges are widely accepted as satisfactory.

Because of our traditional confusion of normal with average, we have come to accept as inevitable that it is normal to suffer increasing symptoms with age. The older you get, the worse you feel, in other words. Yet how can that logically be? Is it normal to have sixty complaints just because you are fifty or sixty years old? We do not think so. In preventive medicine, if you have *one* symptom or complaint we think there is something wrong. You are not well.

The normal person is one who lives his or her entire life without a symptom. One may break a leg in an accident, or

get hit by a car, or even have a few symptoms but nevertheless recover without suffering a clinical disease. It is amazing
to contemplate what is termed a "normal" pregnancy. Often
it includes sickness, fatigue, nausea. These are "average."
They should not occur in a normal, healthy pregnancy.

There is probably a very small percentage of truly normal
people in this country. You may not know anybody who is
totally free of complaints; it seems almost everybody is at
least tired these days. But there have been millions of normal
people in the world, and today there are normal people in
those parts of the world still somewhat protected from so-
called civilization. The inhabitants of Hunza in northern
India live to be 120 and they wouldn't think of *not* working
until they die. They undergo no debilitating senility, no
agonizing arthritis, no fearsome cancer. Men at ninety still
father children, and the women don't go through the menopause until late, and then it is without hot flashes or irritability. One day when they are very old, they just don't wake
up; they die without slow degeneration.

These are normal people.

It is not simply a matter of heredity. People who leave
Hunza begin degenerating. Those who go into Hunza enjoy
increased longevity. Genetics is important, but the life style
of the Hunzakuts is of even greater importance.

Throughout the rest of this book, and ever after, let us
think of normal as being perfectly healthy, without a single
symptom. The chart in Figure 1 gives a visual picture of the
difference between normal and average, in regard to degeneration.

2. *Disease takes a long time to develop.* If this seems obvious, it may surprise you to know that it isn't taken for
granted. You may have heard about the fellow who went to
the doctor for a checkup and was certified as "okay." The
next day—or was it en route home from the doctor's office?—

he was stricken by a heart attack. Now, what the doctor did was to certify that he didn't have a clinical abnormality *at that moment.* There was nothing startling that the stethoscope and electrocardiograph machine, both disease-detection tools, could pick up. But obviously something had been at work inside that patient for a long time; heart disease doesn't appear overnight.

That patient probably had some inkling of his trouble many months or years before it felled him. Another way of stating key number 2 is:

Symptoms appear a long time before a clinical disease is manifested.

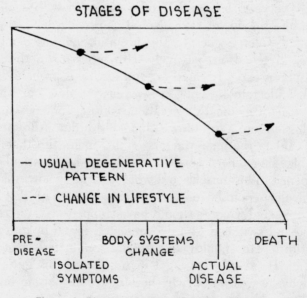

Figure 2. Disease takes a long time to develop

George Clemmons, let's call him, has had a bout of indigestion. It lasts for weeks. Finally he goes to his physician.

"I've got a little heartburn, Doc," he says. The doctor does an upper gastrointestinal series, finds no hole in his duodenum, and reports, "Well, you don't have an ulcer. You're okay."

"Whew," says George. "I'm really relieved. I don't have cancer or an ulcer!"

He still has his heartburn, but because nothing physical has been found in his x-rays he thinks he's all right.

Two years later the heartburn gets worse and he goes back for another GI series. Still no ulcer. In preventive medicine, if he had any symptom he'd be considered abnormal, but in traditional medicine he would still be classified as normal unless he had that hole in his small intestine.

So five years later old George comes in with a bleeding ulcer and the doctor says, "Now I can treat you. You have a disease." George goes to the hospital, spilling blood, and there, stretched out passively with tubes in his throat and veins, he is expertly cared for and his life is probably saved.

That ulcer took many, many years to develop. Through the years of medical observation, waiting for his symptoms to blossom into a full-blown clinical disorder, little attention was paid to the many factors of this man's life that led to the bleeding ulcer: what he ate, what he breathed, what happened to his muscles and what his energy flow was.

The ulcer could have been prevented. When his first symptom appeared, George should have stopped drinking regular coffee and switched to a decaffeinated brand or to a coffee substitute. He should have totally eliminated spices and alcohol. He should have got in touch with his gut: found out why he was upset, why he was keeping his feelings in, and learned how to express his emotions.

Although he was unaware of it, George didn't *get* a bleeding ulcer. George *gave* himself a bleeding ulcer. The same is true for a person who suffers a heart attack; he gives himself a heart attack. In any case of clinical disease, a person's life style determines to a large extent what he *gives* himself and how severely he has done so.

The groundwork for disease may even be laid before a person is conceived. If the parents are not healthy, especially the mother, the child is likely to be weaker, as far as disease resistance is concerned, in the womb and later in life. Malnutrition, for instance, is a condition that makes its effect felt over a long period of time. In dietary analysis, we almost never find a person who ingests all the minimum daily requirements of all the nutrients. That would be at the maintenance level only. This indicates that subclinical nutritional deficiencies are rampant in this country. Possibly fewer than one percent of our people have every single nutrient in their diet.

Disease often takes several decades to develop. If you have any symptoms now, you're working on something. Whether it's heartburn, dental caries, aches of any sort or just plain fatigue, you're degenerating. Fortunately, there is something you can do about it. Now is the time to start. Why wait until you have given yourself a clinical illness?

3. *Susceptibility factors increase the likelihood of disease. Resistance factors lower the possibility of disease.* Have you noticed that some people get a severe case of the flu, some a light case, while others seem to escape it altogether without even the benefit of "flu shots"? It happens every year and for almost every disease you can name. This is primarily the result of host resistance and host susceptibility. Influenza viruses are in the air most of the time during each peak season. The fact that "bugs" cause the disease is only part of the truth. The bug must have a "host" in which to harbor. The host is you—or any patient who comes down with the flu. Mainly because of the incredible advances in antibiotic science during the last decade or so, in modern medicine we

concentrate on wiping out the bug itself as if it existed separately from the patient. This has overshadowed the much more relevant facts:

If a person is truly strong and well, he won't get sick. If he is resistant enough, he won't become susceptible to the illness.

This concept isn't new, though professional medicine has largely ignored it for generations. Perhaps you've heard your grandmother say, "She always has a cold—no resistance at all," or "He never gets sick. He's strong as a bull."

Maybe she told you to go to bed or eat chicken soup when you were ill, to increase your resistance. In her folk wisdom she was aware that if you were strong and healthy, *no* bug would lay you low, and if you weren't, you'd "catch" every one that came along.

The techniques of Human Life Styling all revolve around this concept: how you can learn to build up your resistance factors and thereby lower your susceptibility to illnesses. Resistance is not only one factor. It, like everything else related to your health, is multifarious. All the factors of resistance must be present in order for you to stay well. All of them. If some are missing, then your resistance has been lowered.

Resistance factors are positive, the things you can do to improve your health and well-being. Susceptibility factors are negative, the things you must avoid to keep from degenerating. In Human Life Styling, you accentuate the positive and eliminate the negative.

Let us glance back at the Hunzakut, a normal person. The Hunzakut is very low on susceptibility factors, such as smoking, ingestion of refined foods and saturated fats, lack of exercise and overresponse to stress. At the same time he is very high on resistance factors: he exercises regularly, eats whole, unrefined food and balances his nutrition, enjoys a low stress response to his environment.

Nutrition is particularly important. Everything you eat or drink can be either positive or negative. You need all the essential vitamins, minerals, amino acids and other factors. If any one is missing, you become more susceptible to disease. A British study has shown that an entire group of diseases can be traced to one cause, the high intake of white flour and sugar. Dr. Weston A. Price, in his global, firsthand study of primitive and civilized man, documented with photographs and statistics how modern, refined diets brought degeneration and disease—and damaged the next generation as well. In this country we consume well over one hundred pounds of table sugar per capita annually. Some people consume much more. It is a major susceptibility factor.

The person with perfect resistance is one who gives his body what it needs. By developing his body resistance he can handle the stresses of life better. Instead of breaking under stress, he rolls with the punch or it doesn't faze him. Exposed to cold viruses, he just doesn't get them as often. Exposed to pollution, he withstands that better—although that's a susceptibility factor in itself.

In sum, then, the aim of Human Life Styling is to help you achieve *normal* health, arresting disease in its early stage before it has had time to develop, while diminishing or eliminating your susceptibility factors and increasing your resistance factors. To achieve this, a four-part program has been formulated, which includes these areas:

1. Ecology
2. Nutrition
3. Exercise
4. Stress reduction

A fifth area is that of balancing hormones, cellular enzymes and body energy flow. Because of our biochemical individuality, some people will find this necessary. It is a complex matter that must be supervised by a modern preventive physician who is aware of cellular enzyme function and subclinical illness. Ninety-five percent of all individuals, however, will benefit dramatically from the Human Life Styling program alone; and this book, after all, is about what you can do for yourself. The program can do no harm, so there is absolutely nothing to lose and everything to gain.

Each area of this program—ecology, nutrition, exercise, stress reduction—fits together with the others. They are synergistic, a technical term used to indicate that the whole is greater than the sum of its parts. Put them to work together and their impact will be enhanced.

Mathematically we can express it like this: $1 + 1 + 1 + 1 = 5$ or more.

The more you adhere to proper nutrition, the easier it is to reduce stress. The more you reduce stress, the easier it is to exercise every day. The more exercise you get, the better you will feel and the more able you will be to maintain your programs of nutrition and stress reduction.

The goal of Human Life Styling is to improve the whole human being, not to treat a specific illness. If you have a serious illness, you will have to go to your doctor. However, in the process of following this program almost all diseases "melt" away or at least improve. The four parts working together enable the body to resist disease more effectively and to function more positively—if you are willing to begin now with the idea of changing your health habits for the rest of your life.

As you get into it, you will probably conclude that Human Life Styling is just good common sense. It methodically helps you to do what you already know, down deep, that you ought to do.

Which, in a world where human beings have lost touch with themselves, can be a revolutionary experience.

2

The Four Horsemen of Health

Would you like to know how to avoid heart disease? And stroke? And the equally dread disease cancer?

It's not as difficult as you might think, nor is it so mysterious as we have been led to suspect. There are enough medical data already available so that we can program ourselves to keep free of these diseases. We can make use of those data to prevent the conditions. It's a matter of life styles.

Let's begin with the number one mass killer today.

How to Avoid Heart Disease

When a patient comes into a doctor's office, it is possible to predict within a 10 percent margin his or her risk of suffering a coronary attack. Once the extent of the danger is known, the patient can be instructed as to how to lower the risk.

This is not an extravagant claim. It is already known what causes coronaries. The subject has been studied from every angle by research teams. The correlation factors have been added up. From all this data, most of them statistical, we can with great accuracy describe the medical "profile" of the coronary-prone individual.

Let's do a "quickie" profile right now, to give you the general idea. You can compute your own risk factors. The total will give you a rough approximation of how you stand. It will not be precise. For simplicity's sake we have rounded out the percentages.

Go down the list and give yourself 10 points each time you qualify as being in a particular risk category. Write down the figures on a piece of paper. The sum will be your total percentage risk for a coronary.

1. Male and over thirty-five years of age, or female and over sixty. We can do nothing about this one. If you are a female under sixty or a male under thirty-five you can note 0.

From now on, age and sex will not be a factor.

2. Cigarette smoking. (If you don't smoke cigarettes, 0. If you smoke a pipe or cigar, or if you've stopped smoking within the last five years, the risk is somewhere between 0 and 10, but we are rounding off figures to keep it simple.)

3. Anything but thin.

4. No regular exercise. ("Regular" means at least five days a week; to earn a 0 you must work up a sweat for at least twenty minutes, five days a week; stretching exercises, week-end golf or sitting in the sauna several times a week won't get you off the hook.)

5. Feeling tense a great deal of the time. (Admittedly a vague thing, but important.)

6. Depressions and feelings of inadequacy much of the time. (Not just on rare occasions.)

7. A history of one or more persons in your family who has had a coronary or stroke before reaching sixty.

8. Consumption of any of the following: refined carbohydrates (sugar, white starch, doughnuts, sweets), junk meats

(frankfurters, lunch meats, hamburgers), coffee, saturated animal fats.

9. Blood cholesterol level higher than 240 milligrams percent. (If you don't know, give yourself 5 points, to be sure.)

10. Blood sugar level over 120 milligrams percent or under 70, two hours after test began. If you don't know, make it 5 points anyway.

11. Uric acid over 6.5. If you don't know, 5 points.

12. Elevated blood pressure (138/88 or higher).

Theoretically, a person could add up more than 100 points on this test. It was purposely designed that way, not only for convenience in counting but also to emphasize the high risk status a person has if he or she combines many of the factors. Nevertheless, it provides a swift general means of assessing your own future health in this one respect.

How did you do on the test? If your score was low, take ten minutes to rejoice, and continue your good health habits. If it was high, you can start today to do something about it. You can't change your sex or age or family history, but you *can* change your medical history so that your children and grandchildren and their children will have better odds. Almost every factor cited is related to diet and exercise, and some to stress reduction—factors which you can directly control.

By using these general guidelines you can predict your own illness, which means you can direct the course of the illness. You can choose to have a coronary or you can choose not to have one. It's up to you. God does not give you a coronary. It is man-made.

This is fortunate. The individual can do something about his plight. Let's say the person is a stocky, overweight male who smokes and gets no exercise. He can't change the fact of his maleness, but he can eliminate his obesity, he can stop smoking and he can start exercising. By doing so, he reduces his risk from perhaps 90 percent to somewhere under 30 percent. In effect, he has prevented an almost certain coronary.

Coronary heart disease, as befits our major killer, has been one of the most researched physical conditions. The Framingham, Massachusetts, study under the direction of the National Institute of Health is probably the best known. It is based on thousands of patients over a twenty-year period. It answers a basic question: Who gets coronaries and who does not? Because coronary heart disease has been examined more carefully than most other diseases, its statistical prediction is one of the most accurate. One person, for example, might do everything wrong, medically speaking, and live to be eighty, a pretty good age. But when a thousand or more persons are studied, a statistical pattern forms, and that one person is seen as the exception.

In the Framingham study, the people who predominantly suffered coronaries were males who were overweight, consumed a large amount of sugar and white starch, took no exercise and smoked. Also on the list was the consumption of saturated fats, which was believed to be very important. In fact, much of the assault on heart disease has centered around the cholesterol factor, which saturated fats are believed to increase in the bloodstream; the total picture has received relatively little attention.

But who *didn't* get coronaries? It was like turning the question inside out. Data indicated that those who were exempt were slender, didn't smoke, exercised, and ate no sugar, white starch and saturated fats.

In other words, do just the opposite of what gives you a coronary and you will improve your health. It comes down to a change in life styles, an exchanging of resistance factors for susceptibility factors.

In our "quickie" profile for your benefit, we simplified the risk factors enormously; perhaps even oversimplified them. So let's look at the individual variables and see what they mean statistically. Isolating each risk factor, we find that at age forty a man has five times more chance of giving himself a heart attack if he is overweight. If he does absolutely no exercise, his dangers are six times those of a man who takes a short walk every day. Those who regularly do aerobic exercises—sustained walking, running, swimming, biking—may lower their risks as much as *one hundred times*. On the other hand, smoking increases your risk from four to eight times. And the person with a 300 milligram blood cholesterol reading has ten times the risk of a person with a 200 reading.

One study has revealed a relationship between coronary heart disease and emotional stress. The overachievers, those who set time goals for themselves and are rigid and not relaxed, have an 80 percent correlation with heart attacks. This study showed a risk rate that was eight to twenty times higher among those who overrespond to stress. Again this is a factor that can be changed by the individual himself.

The main thing to consider, above all, is the overall picture. Cholesterol, for example, does correlate with arteriosclerosis, but that is only part of the matter. Earlier it was assumed that if the person didn't take in cholesterol through his food he would be all right. Unfortunately, it isn't that simple. Only about 10 percent of your serum cholesterol comes from what you eat. The other 90 percent is manufactured in the body from saturated fats and excessive refined carbohydrates—that is to say, white starch and sugar. It is now known that there are five types of people, classified as to how they handle the fat-protein complexes. If you're a Type IV, for example, any kind of carbohydrate will raise your cholesterol and triglycerides. Generally, eating eggs will not raise your cholesterol level; some doctors have found eggs to be a possible factor in lowering cholesterol levels in the blood. However, if you are a Type II as far as handling lipoproteins is concerned, you may be one who shouldn't eat eggs. The main thing to remember is that this is just one part, one part of many, and it shouldn't be allowed to obscure the whole picture.

By attending to the whole, we can do something besides wait and pray that nothing goes wrong. Coronary heart disease is almost 100 percent preventable. Now, this is not to say that if a person's arteries are already calcified they will return to perfectly normal, but at least they will tend toward normal, which is a vast improvement. Even after a heart attack, a person may use Human Life Styling to prevent a recurrence.

Let's take the illustration of an actual patient who followed the Human Life Styling program. Since he did not have a heart attack, we cannot say for certain that he was headed for one, but all the signposts strongly indicated it.

Eugene Smart at fifty was a successful stockbroker. He was a prime example of the person who has no major complaints but is in a very high risk category for coronary heart disease, stroke or other illnesses.

His main complaint was that he slept poorly and was quite nervous. He was somewhat overweight and his blood pressure was slightly elevated. Previously a doctor had assured him that these were "nothing serious" and that he was "in excellent health."

However, his uric acid level was also a little high, his cholesterol reading was over 250, and the electrocardiogram (EKG) indicated some very minor changes. These, too, he had been earlier told, were "within normal limits."

A dietary analysis was made of his eating habits; the results were graded by a computer. Eugene Smart was consuming the equivalent of forty teaspoonsful of sugar per day. His diet verged on malnutrition. He took no vitamin or mineral supplements.

He was getting no exercise at all, and although he enjoyed his work, he allowed it to induce an extreme state of stress in himself.

In sum, he was in the high risk group for coronary. He may have been "average" for his age, but he was far from normal.

He started immediately to improve his nutrition, exercise and stress response. He ate more raw foods, eliminated sugar and began a weight-control program. He stopped drinking ten cups of coffee a day and took calcium, magnesium, vitamins C and E, in addition to a general vitamin supplement. He initiated a regular exercise plan.

He immediately began sleeping well, which solved his major complaint right off. Even though he had the same sources of stress at his work, he was much less nervous. He could handle it now. His weight gradually went down.

What was most significant of all, along with his improvement in specific symptoms he now was dropping toward the 20 percent risk group, moving safely away from his previous 80 percent risk classification.

In contrast to Eugene Smart's sensible preventive approach to health, let's take the cases of two other patients. One woman, a diabetic with high blood pressure, knew she was not supposed to consume salt or sweets. But because it was a holiday, she was eating fried chicken and apple pie like mad. She suffered a coronary. Another patient, a sixty-eight-year-old man, played several sets of tennis every Saturday afternoon, although he had been repeatedly admonished to play a single set every day instead. And he was told to do his aerobic exercises. He didn't. He suffered a coronary. Both of them had given themselves heart attacks.

They could have followed Eugene Smart's example and

enjoyed pleasant health outside the walls of the intensive care unit. Making positive changes in a life style helps to ensure that people don't drop dead of coronaries within a week after a checkup.

. . . And Stroke

A stroke is a cerebral vascular accident. It is similar to a coronary attack in that it is a disease of the blood vessels, which have become occluded. A clot forms to shut off the blood supply to the brain, or else blood flows out and causes bleeding in the brain. Whichever way it happens, the nervous system's blood supply is impaired.

Who suffer strokes?

Here women do not have the edge of safety they hold on men in coronary heart disease. Stroke seems to strike male and female about equally. Age, however, is a factor. It occurs mostly in older people. If you are over sixty, you are in a higher risk group. Hereditary factors must also be considered.

There is nothing we can do about our age or our heredity, so let's see if there is something we *can* change.

High blood pressure is high on the risk-factor list for stroke. We can do something about that. And there are other factors: overweight, sugar and white starch, saturated fats, overwork, smoking, lack of exercise, overresponse to stress, diabetes, high serum cholesterol, and other fats called triglycerides.

Exactly how a stroke develops we don't know. We only know that people with these factors in their life styles are likely to have strokes. By knowing what the factors are and avoiding them, you start preventing stroke.

Does this sound familiar? It seems as if we had just boiled down some of the paragraphs from the section on heart disease, doesn't it? Stroke, in other words, is caused by the same, or almost the same, factors. They are not in the same sequence as in heart disease, but the same factors of resistance and susceptibility do crop up in both disorders.

Now let us discuss an illness that most people consider to be an act of God, about which nothing can be done.

How to Avoid Cancer

In eighteenth-century England, one segment of the population was plagued by cancer of the scrotum. Who were they? Young chimney sweeps. Why? Well, it turned out to be directly linked to their occupation. Unbathed, the youths lived for weeks at a time in the same crotch-tight, soot-lined clothes. Their life style brought carcinogens into intimate contact with the tissues where the cancer developed. Once these conditions were related to the disease by a perceptive observer, the London Town Council began to regulate the boys' hygiene, requiring soap-and-water baths at specific intervals. The mandatory change in life style brought an end to the scrotal cancer epidemic.

This was not early detection and treatment; it was true prevention. Prevention was achieved simply by changing their life styles. This is true for most cancers, perhaps for all.

Today the Pap smear for women is one of the most effective means of early cancer detection we have. It enables the pathologist to detect uterine cancer cells in their earliest stages, so that the condition can be treated energetically before it spreads. Every woman should have one regularly, at least once a year—even very young women. It is an excellent early detection technique.

But it does not prevent cancer. If you are a woman reading this, can you recall what the doctor told you after your last Pap smear? Did he tell you how to keep from getting cancer?

No, he simply took the smear, as all of us do, and prayed along with you that the lab results would be negative—until your next visit.

But, as with heart disease and stroke, there is a great deal of knowledge about the factors that correlate highly with incidence of cancer in general. It is possible to advise people how to lower their chances of getting it.

In addition to general risk factors, there are other life style factors that figure in cancer incidence at specific sites. These are parallel in many ways to the chimney sweeps' scrotal cancers. Let's look at several of these cancers.

Cervical or uterine cancer may strike any woman, but her chances of having it rise or fall in proportion to a number of factors related to sexual life style. Particular factors that lead to high risk for this cancer include youthful onset of coitus, multiple sexual partners, non-circumcision of the male partner, first pregnancy while a teen-ager, multiple pregnancies under age twenty. A gynecologist could determine part of a patient's risk group with a few simple questions, coordinated with an investigation of her intake of additives, nutritional status, exercise and stress.

Once a woman has already become part of a high risk group for cervical cancer, there are, nonetheless, a number of things she, like the rest of us, can do to lower her cancer risks. The same steps that can be taken to prevent cancer in another part of the body can be used against cervical cancer.

Before examining these resistance factors, however, let's look at some other specific cancer problems. Cancer of the esophagus is one of the most distressing. It is more deadly than lung cancer, primarily because it is often detected too late; by the time the patient's symptoms push him to the doctor's office the cancer has usually spread too far to be controlled. Thus, prospects for cure of esophageal cancer are grim. It can, however, be prevented.

How? First, let's look at the correlation factors for cancer of the esophagus. There are four of them: smoking, drinking of alcoholic beverages, long-term nutritional deficiency, and esophageal irritation (drinking beverages or eating food that is too hot; in Asia, betel chewing). The two major risk factors are smoking and alcohol. It doesn't matter whether the smoking involves cigarettes, cigars or pipes; the alcohol can be anything from beer to whiskey. Smoking and drinking, period. The two make a cancerous combination.

These data provide the obvious answer. To prevent cancer of the esophagus, do not smoke, do not drink alcoholic beverages, avoid malnutrition to any degree and avoid repeated irritation of the esophagus. These are all life style factors.

Another cancer that has claimed many lives is that of the colon. There is almost directly a correlation of three things in bowel cancer: obesity, constipation and the consumption of nitrates. Nitrates are chemical additives used as preservatives in lunch meats, frankfurters and such foods. In the body the nitrates are changed into deadly carcinogens, which during constipation come into prolonged contact with bowel tissue. Bowel disorders have also been linked to consumption of sugar and white flour, both of which may be factors in causing constipation. Overprocessed foods have a lower fiber content, for one thing; a high fiber content helps prevent constipation.

The factors, then, are known. If you want to avoid cancer of the colon, you lower your risk tremendously by doing three things: don't let yourself get constipated, don't eat foods with nitrates in them, and lose weight. And usually if you exercise, drink enough fluids and eat fresh, whole food, you won't have the problems of constipation and obesity.

By now, in viewing these specific kinds of cancer, you will see that a person's life style is vitally relevant to whether he or she is stricken with cancer. If we kept on with our review until we had studied every site in the body where cancer may appear, we would soon begin seeing a *cluster* of correlation factors. Some that we have mentioned already would start reappearing in other cancers. Finally an overall pattern would form.

When all the high correlation factors had been added up, the result would be something like this: Who gets cancer? People who are overweight, who have an increased intake of sugar and processed foods containing additives, who respond excessively to stress and have feelings of inadequacy and repressed rage, who take no exercise, who smoke, who drink coffee and alcohol excessively. For instance, the heavy smoker's chance of developing lung cancer may be one hundred times greater than that of a nonsmoker, and the risk rises with the number of cigarettes he smokes each day. But not recognized by many people is the fact that the smoker has a ten to thirty times greater risk of getting other kinds of cancer than does a nonsmoker. Some disability of the lungs is inevitable for the smoker. *Everyone* who smokes gets emphysema; the degree depends on how long and how much he smokes.

The person's response to stress is highly important. One study showed that people who did not repress their rage or fear just never got cancer. Over 95 percent of people with cancer who were studied in this respect showed themselves to be emotionally repressed.

Now, these are practically the same factors that correlated with heart disease and stroke. The emphasis is different in each of the three diseases, but the same factors keep cropping up.

In fact, so many of these same factors appear in so many diseases that Dr. Emanuel Cheraskin has suggested that we just call the preclinical symptoms a "syndrome of sickness." Which direction the disease takes later should be of less interest to us than what we can do now to head it off.

And again, as was pointed out earlier, we can prevent cancer by avoiding the risk factors that correlate most strikingly with the incidence of cancer. Don't smoke. Keep thin. Eat raw, unrefined foods. Shun sugar and white flour. Avoid risky additives. Learn to respond properly to stress. Express your emotions openly; don't bottle them up.

Exercise is possibly the top resistance factor in warding off cancer. Those who exercise properly and regularly are *much* less susceptible to cancer. Exactly why this seems to be so is not known, but if you need a theory to explain it, there is one. In fact, there are many, many theories about cancer, which is why we merely present this one without certifying its validity. It would explain, however, why sedentary, overweight people are more susceptible to cancer.

Essentially the view is this: Every one of us produces an estimated three to three hundred mutagenic, potentially cancerous, cells each day. In the individual who is obese or who gets no exercise, there is a sludging effect in the precapillaries, the area where the arteries narrow down to join relatively minute vessels. This sludging allows the wild cancer cell to dig in and take hold, eventually reproducing and extending its control until it comes to clinical notice.

Now, if the person exercises and is not overweight, sludging does not occur. We still manufacture those potential cancer cells every day, but with a healthy circulatory system they are taken care of, probably by the phagocytes, which are the scavengers, or clean-up cells, of the bloodstream, or they may be eliminated by the protein enzymes that circulate in the blood if we don't eat too much protein. (If we overeat on protein, this may result in an increased burden for these particular enzymes.)

As interesting as this theory is, it remains speculatory. Actually it is relatively unimportant whether it is true or not. What is important is that exercise and thinness help guard against cancer, whatever the process.

One part of the process, by whatever name, appears to be resistance. If every one of us produces malignant cells in our bodies every day, why doesn't everybody get cancer? The most logical answer seems to be related to individual resistance, as well as susceptibility factors.

The story of Charlie Koppla, while by no means typical, beautifully illustrates what may occur in a rare instance. He was a zealous businessman with every possible deleterious physical habit, as far as health was concerned. At age forty-five Charlie learned he had cancer of the colon.

He had an operation. He was told he did not have long to live. So he quit his business. He didn't really like it anyway. Even his social situation was stressful; he gladly gave that up, too. He began to do what he had always wanted to do: he went to the South Seas and bought a boat. In the process he found a great tranquillity in himself. He is still alive, fifteen years later.

How did he outlive the prediction? He changed his life style. He shed excessive stress, he had a better diet, he began living in the open air and he exercised regularly.

The doctors handling his case called it "spontaneous regression." "For reasons unknown, some cancers just go away," they say. But Charlie Koppla knew it had something to do with the revolutionary changes in his life.

There is no point in waiting as long as Charlie did before building up your resistance. The really optimistic thing is that we don't have to find out exactly how cancer—and other diseases—start, in order to save lives.

Cancer predictability is between 60 and 80 percent reliable. That's pretty good for a disease most people think is an act of God, uncontrollable by the patient and virtually incurable by the physician.

The Four Horsemen of Health

As we analyze the three diseases in this chapter, we find that the major correlation factors in all of them will fit into these categories: nutrition, exercise, stress reduction. Evaluation of these three can be used to predict illness years before it is clinical activity. In the body, all the cells are related to each other and therefore anything you do, or don't do, in these three areas will affect, directly or indirectly, every cell in your body. You might think of it as body ecology. The fourth factor in your health is the environment.

We also find that the three treacherous clinical diseases—heart disease, stroke and cancer—have risk factors in common. In other words, the same things will place you in a high risk group for all three of these diseases—and a number of others, too. The truth is, as we have tried to demonstrate here with three of our biggest killers, that *most illnesses can be caused by the same factors.* The risk factors are not in the same sequence of importance for every disease, but they are there, somewhere on the list. For instance, carcinogenic food additives are likely to be more important in cancer than in coronary disease. High blood pressure is more important to stroke than to other diseases. But most of these factors crop up in each illness, to some degree.

Obviously, then, there are certain factors that are good for people and certain factors that are bad for most people. Our bodies have evolved to handle the ingredients, actions and stresses of a certain way of life. The more our bodies are in tune with that physical heritage, the healthier we will be, individually and as a species.

In medicine we have become obsessed with the idea that for one disease there is one treatment. This attitude tends to ignore the reality that disease is occurring in a *person*. For some reason, that body wasn't working right in which disease occurred. Yet we sometimes carry the view to such lengths that the treatment becomes worse than the illness itself. A cold, for example, is not one of the killer diseases. Yet the battery of drugs that are used merely to control congestion is amazing.

What is especially significant here is a discovery by Dr. Hans Selye, who showed that the body responds to all stresses in a similar manner. He termed this the General Adaptation Syndrome. The body's response works first through the hypothalamus, which is in the midbrain, and thence through the pituitary gland, which activates the adrenal glands, which in turn have many influences on the entire body. No matter what the form of stress is, the body reacts in a general way. This is true whether it is a cold virus, a cancer cell or emotional stress.

In other words, if you are under stress, your body is degenerating. Hard as it is to get across, the concept is a very simple one.

Both doctors and patients, trained to think in terms of a specific disease when symptoms appear, would be better off to look upon any complaint that's not normal functioning as a syndrome of sickness, to use Cheraskin's term. Why wait to name the disease when it is general and has the same apparent factors of degeneration of the body? It is more effective to look upon a complaint as the end result of susceptibility factors, which should be avoided totally. Any laxity at all regarding susceptibility factors is simply poisoning the body and should be recognized as doing so. Then the person, charged with this knowledge, has the option to poison himself if he wishes, for he clearly knows the consequences. By the same token, parents can decide whether or not to poison their children and leave them with the consequences of an array of susceptibility factors.

How is disease avoided? The key is in methodically changing your life style. The changes must be consistent and lifelong, not effected temporarily or sporadically. Proof has long been accumulating as to the role of a person's life style in determining health. Let us look at several recent examples.

When researchers years ago were searching for *the* cause of heart disease, it appeared that the trouble had been traced to dietary animal fats. High-fat diets brought on heart disease —except in the Eskimo. The Eskimo had one of the most fat-rich diets on earth. A diet of whale blubber is obviously rich in fat. But the Eskimo didn't have heart disease. Why? Well, the speculation ranged far, but now it seems apparent that the Eskimo's entire life style was protecting him from this disease of "civilized" man.

Recently, however, in two very important ways, the Eskimo has tended toward "modernization" and hence toward some of the physical problems associated with the process. The "civilized" diet of refined and processed foods is accompanied by the use of labor-saving devices such as snow machines and chain saws. The Eskimo, in going off his natural diet and the vigorous exercise that protected him against heart disease for centuries, is becoming overweight and already seems to be tending toward a glucose—or sugar—intolerance that may be an early trend toward diabetes. When a life style degenerates, so does the person.

Though the present-day plight of the Eskimo is discouraging, there is hope. If they go back to their old life style, they can return to normal. The impact of life style has been demonstrated in Dr. McCamy's own clinic. In one study of thirty-five young executives and professors, the chief complaint was chest pain and fatigue, but more serious, coronary problems were suspected. The subjects ranged in age from twenty-five to forty and all but one were male. Their resting electrocardiograms (EKG) were normal and they had no very high cholesterol readings, yet each had tense chest muscles. Why? An investigation into their life styles showed the pattern. More than thirty of them smoked. They averaged an intake of ten cups of coffee or tea daily. They all suffered from poor posture. They all overworked, putting in twelve to twenty hours a day. They had no exercise. They all had very unsatisfactory diets. They were bending over most of the day. Every one of these points was a matter of life style and each one was a susceptibility factor.

They were introduced to Human Life Styling. They stopped drinking coffee, alcohol; they stopped eating spices and heavy fried foods. Those who smoked cut down to less than a pack a day, with the ultimate goal in mind of quitting completely. They reduced their workday. They introduced stretching exercises into their routines and initiated walking programs.

Every single one of them stopped having chest pains.

Which clinical disease had they been headed toward? It's difficult to say. We called it the "young professional chest syndrome." Some could have been diagnosed as having pleurisy, heartburn, early arthritis or muscle spasms. In a way, these labels are meaningless, however, for all the patients really had a chronic stress reaction. We are back to the General Adaptation Syndrome that Hans Selye discovered.

Like many other patients who suffered from fatigue for a long time, once they began the Human Life Styling program they felt better, thought more clearly, were happier and felt less tired. If the pains returned, it was because the patient had discontinued one of the elements of the program.

Another study involved forty upper-middle-class women. All had already been to reputable physicians, but not one had ever had a dietary survey taken. Now they filled out dietary questionnaires, which were graded by a computer, and they wrote down their precise eating habits on seven-day diet sheets. The results were astounding. Approximately 25 percent of them suffered from a total protein deficiency, while 75 percent were deficient in one or more amino acids. (Amino acids are protein factors.) Those who were malnourished changed their diets and did better. With exercise added, they improved even more. Working on stress factors enhanced the total effect.

In the clinic it was observed that less than 10 percent of patients have even the minimal daily requirement of every single nutritional factor in their diet. The well-nourished American is a myth. Anybody who disagrees should be prepared to report how many dietary analyses he or she has done lately.

Fatigue and any chest pains are early warnings. A clinical case of heart murmur or ulcer is a very late finding. Disease starts way back, sometimes decades before it erupts into a precise clinical diagnosis. Invariably a total evaluation of the patient reveals a deficiency in all three major areas of nutrition, exercise and stress response.

In order to attain total improvement, you must work in all three areas. Failure to do anything in one area will tend to weaken your efforts in another. It's like the man who is taking vitamin E but still smoking, or is eating organic food but not exercising. You can't "just eat right" and maximize your health. You can't "just exercise" and maximize your health. Certainly it will help, but you need the whole program together, all at once.

The goal is to become normal by doing what is normal for the human body. It is normal for humans to walk, run, swim and bike. Our bodies are kinetically evolved. It is abnormal for us *not* to walk twenty minutes a day. If you think, "But I don't have time to walk twenty minutes a day," the truth is that you're leading an abnormal life.

Breathing fresh air deeply into your lungs is normal. It is abnormal to breathe 200 degrees of poisonous chemical fumes into your body, as you do in smoking cigarettes. No other animal does such a thing. And so the list goes.

Some people argue that, well, exercise is the main thing. Others say the avoidance of sugar is what we must emphasize. But the truth is that all factors are important. The facts are very clear. Why argue over which one is more important? Each needs the others, and you need all of them.

Once you have got what we call the four horsemen of health pulling for you, you will realize what we call the "spiral effect." The spiral effect works both ways. If you gorge yourself with food, you don't feel like taking a walk. The less walking you do, the more you want to stuff and the more lethargic you get. The more lethargic you become, the less conscious you are of your inner needs, the more you want to eat and the less exercise you want to take; you spiral downward. Both psyche and body degenerate in the spiral of discouragement.

But you can break that cycle. Start exercising, after you read the pertinent chapter; whether you want to or not, do your aerobics regularly. Don't think about it—do it. Do the same with your eating pattern; eat the foods you should, when you should. Don't think about it—just do it. Work on your stress-reduction program, doing each day what you can. This is when you start spiraling upward. As you eat good food and avoid the hostile food, your body will feel better and will operate more efficiently. You won't mind the exercise as much as you did. Your head will feel better; you won't feel so depressed. You take another spiral upward.

As a species we haven't really evolved much in the last

ten thousand years. This means our bodies are basically ten thousand years old, maybe a hundred thousand, a relatively brief period of time for such things. That's back to the hunting and gathering stage of man's development. Remember that our bodies are there, despite our overveneered civilization. Our bodies were never meant to consume refined sugar. Our bodies were designed to eat simple, natural foods. We just don't have the metabolic equipment to do otherwise in an efficient manner. Our bodies were never meant to undergo the continuous stresses and conflicts of modern life.

You don't have to return to the hunting stage. But you can care for your body as well as your hunter ancestor cared for his. That hunter was a whole person. Modern man has become fragmented. The body and the mind are one. They cannot be separated. If you're not doing what's right for the body, you're not doing what's right for the whole person. It all has to fit together.

A Mental Trip Before You Start

To get a clearer picture of what the good, natural life is, let's take a little trip in our imaginations. Have someone read the next several paragraphs to you—slowly.

First, sit comfortably with your back relatively straight against the wall or in a straight chair. If it's comfortable enough for you, you may sit in the middle of the room. Or if you prefer, lie on the floor. Put your hands together or by your sides.

Now close your eyes and then take a deep breath. Fill your lungs full, then freely exhale. All the way out—and out and out. Then another slow, full breath in and then out fully. Keep breathing slowly and rhythmically. Become aware of your breath passing from the outside, through the nasal passages, into the throat, the windpipe and into the lungs. Be aware of the oxygen going through the lungs, into the red blood cells, circulating through your body and into the cells. Feel this a few times. Then be aware of the oxygen, the toxins and the carbon dioxide being carried by the red cells into the lungs and then back out through the windpipe, the throat, the nasal passages and the nostrils, and finally out to the environment.

When does the outside air become you? Is it when it's in the nasal passages? Is when it is in the throat? In the lungs? Or the cells? Or did it ever become you?

And when does the air that was inside you become the environment? When it leaves the cells? When it leaves the lungs? Or when it passes through the nasal passages?

Begin to feel that the air is both you and the environment. You are the same thing. The same air has been breathed by many people, by many fishes, and it has been in many clouds. You are part of the whole environment. It is a part of you.

Now visualize a natural human being at his best in a natural environment that is best for him. Visualize what he is doing, and eating and drinking. How is he spending his day? What thoughts does he have? Stay with him for a while.

[Wait several minutes here before going on.]

Now when you feel like it, take a few deep breaths and full exhales, and open your eyes and come back. Ask yourself pointed questions about what you saw. Did you see colas and hot dogs being eaten? Or any other junk foods being gulped down? Did you see someone sitting all day and never exercising? Did you see anyone breathing in 200-degree fumes with his cigarettes?

Probably you did not see any of those things. You probably saw a person working regularly, walking a lot, breathing fresh air, drinking fresh water, eating fresh, natural foods.

You probably saw him being very happy. Hundreds of patients have been on this trip. None has ever seen anyone eating hot dogs or drinking soda pop. This seems to indicate that inside you there is a natural knowledge of what is best for the human being. We know it, but we have forgotten what is natural for our human bodies. We have lost the joy and rhythm of being fulfilled human beings in touch with our environment.

Well, you may react, the person I saw was in an unspoiled valley. It was natural and simple for him, but we are in the urbanized twentieth century. We are bombarded constantly with different things to do and with so many different opinions.

This is where Human Life Styling comes in: to simplify things for you.

As you read the following chapters, remember that the basic program is one of sequence. Keep it all in proper sequence and you not only can make it work for yourself but you can teach it to others. The main thing is to concentrate on the basic aspects of the program. Where health programs are concerned, so many people wander off into the woods of details. Keep to the basics. Don't let yourself be sidetracked by minutiae.

You will see the program starting to succeed when you begin developing a regular pattern. Whatever you *can* do, you do. Start doing something in each area. Remember that is what it takes to spiral upward. Don't try to do everything at once if you don't want to, but start doing *some* of the things in *each* of the next four chapters.

As a parting tip, start out simply in each of the four sections. Check yourself monthly and annually. Write down the habits that we will recommend.

Someone must monitor your progress if you are to get the most out of the program. You can do it yourself or you can have a friend or a member of your family do it, by examining your Human Life Styling sheet.

Don't be disappointed if there are setbacks. This can be expected at times. Just remember that the goal is a general spiral upward over a long period of time. You are working on a life style, not an instant panacea. A setback for a week or a month is no problem in the greater context of a lifetime, if you continue to work for general improvement.

In the next four chapters we have presented charts and outlines for each of the aspects of Human Life Styling. Remember most of all that the four parts are synergistic and that they work together toward a spiraling upward effect. Assuming that you earn the optimal 30 points in each section, your total points then would not be 120, which would be the simple sum. Instead, if you earn 30 points in each of the four, you will deserve a total of 200 points. It may not be good math, but it's good health! And if you don't like to bother with figures, you can skip the point system in all but the section on exercise. There you *must* keep count of your weekly points.

Approach it simply. Don't let it get too complicated. If you're a point or two off here and there, it doesn't make that much difference. Just keep it up from now on. Many people know what they ought to do, but don't do it. *Do* something every day. In the critical years ahead, we will need our health more than anything else, more than ever before. To do this we will have to get back in touch with our natural rhythms and learn to look forward eagerly to each new day.

So far, we have emphasized three aspects of the Human Life Styling program—nutrition, exercise and stress reduction. Add to these ecology—an active concern for our environment and social involvement in its betterment.

What's the good of being healthy if we don't have a decent world to be healthy in?

3

Ecological You

"How can I, just one individual, do anything about the environmental crisis, when the problems are not only massive but global?"

Don't feel alone if you've asked yourself that. It's enough to make anyone feel insignificant. Our ecological predicament has been documented by books, newspapers, television, magazines and radio almost to the saturation point. We have been inundated by data. For that reason we're not going to overwhelm you again with a Niagara of details. We'll assume you are aware of the problems and agree that something must be done about them.

We do want to point out, briefly, how the environment and your personal health are intimately related, and we want to show you in this chapter two ways you *can* do something about this crisis. These break down into:

1. What you can do by yourself.
2. What you can do by working with others.

The check list at the end of this chapter suggests a number of specific things that you can do by yourself. Performing as many of these actions as you can is like casting a daily vote for the environment in a never-ending election.

By your actions, your words and your influence you become more than one person acting alone. Every one of us has a sphere of influence. What you *do* influences to some extent your family, your friends and the people you come into contact with every day. Review the check list regularly to remind yourself of what you can do. Perhaps you can think of other specific aspects of your ecological life style that you can change. Without the help of anyone else, you can write to your congressman or your mayor or your local newspaper about specific environmental problems. Be an example of what one person can do.

The easiest way to work with others is to join an existing organization. It may be local or national, though it would be ideal to join both. In the more locally oriented organization it is easier to see the results of your work; as part of a large national movement you can have a major impact. In the appendix we have listed several national organizations.

Once you have become aware of your sphere of influence, you can get others involved. Send your congressman, your senators and other political leaders copies of *Replenish the Earth* by G. Tyler Miller, Jr., and *The Limits to Growth* by Donella Meadows et al. Both these books on the environmental crisis are in paperback. Alerting others is an achievement in itself.

It is a time to be involved, as never before in your life.

By now it is obvious that the air is more than a personal, free commodity about which we need not think. It is essential and, most of all, it is shared by all of us in common. If someone else is in the room with you now, you're sharing the breath of life with that person. You do the same on a street, in a car or on a plane. The pollution in the air eventually becomes part of you, entering your lungs and your bloodstream. That's as personal as anything can get. The carbon monoxide levels are high enough in some cities to contribute to heart attacks in people who already have heart or respiratory problems. Pesticides from the soil and water make their way into our food. The average person now has about twelve parts per million of DDT in his or her tissue fat, and DDT is only one of many insecticides. Chemical additives in food grown on depleted soil only increase our personal burdens.

Your involvement with the natural environment is inescapable. How you live and what you do—your life style—inevitably have an impact, either directly or indirectly, on the world around you. If you drive a car, for instance, you contribute to the pollution of the air. Conversely, you are a daily victim of ecological malfunctioning that, to some degree, takes its toll on your body. Just as every cell within us is a part of our total body ecology, so each of us is a small part of the total global environment.

In the closed world system in which we live, the actions of one person have more impact than ever before in history. One individual burning his trash in his backyard can foul the air for an entire community. Because we are crowded on this earth today, a negative act such as that has a magnified effect that would not have been possible, say, fifty years ago. On the other hand, one person can have a positive influence by sharing a car pool, planting a backyard garden fertilized by compost or recycling his household waste products.

There are four broad areas in which individuals, groups and governments must become active if we are to have a healthful world. These needs embrace the major ecological concerns facing us today. They are:

- Slowing down and stopping material growth.
- Conserving and recycling our resources.
- Phasing out pollution.
- Stabilizing population.

In one way or another, each of these four areas affects the quality of our lives. The quality of life is difficult to measure, but there are indexes, such as the amount of mental illness in a society, the suicide rate, the amount of living space per capita, the prevalence of degenerative diseases, the crime rate, accidents and pollution. Based on these, our quality of life is declining all over the world.

Of these four areas of concern, population increase and material growth rank highest in importance. They are practically the same, like two sides of one coin, and they in turn generate the companion problems of pollution and resource depletion. The more the population grows, the more we use our natural resources, grow economically and pollute—and the less there is for each person. The more we grow materially, the more we pollute and exhaust our nonrenewable resources.

The energy crisis that began in 1973 was only an early symptom of our planet's overall malaise. *Material growth must cease*. There is a limit to both land and natural resources. Big is not better. Having more people in your city, your state or your country is no longer a fact to be proud of. Furthermore, the problem is worldwide. Instead of bringing the good life to everyone, material growth will inevitably widen the gap between the rich and the poor countries, leading to war or equally devastating disaster.

The ultimate disease is war. If man destroys the world in a nuclear war, all our work toward personal self-regeneration will have been for naught. This is why we should also work for peace. Help perpetuate the race of man past the next twenty years. Besides affording you an opportunity to be healthy, it will make you feel better to know that your life is part of a solution.

In a simpler time, in a less crowded world, we didn't have to face these, our most urgent, crises. Man has always been an extension of the earth, one part of the entire natural environment, but he was not always forced to acknowledge it. Today, however, the material goals of the past are archaic and invalid because we are in a drastically changed situation. *We have approached the limits to growth on this planet, and we have nowhere else to go.*

This has happened because we are in the upper stages of exponential growth, a phenomenon making its impact for the first time in history. Another way of expressing this is to call it the J-curve concept. It is central to every environmental problem we are having, and with each new crisis symptom it spells out one chilling, monumental warning:

We are now in an entirely new ball game, and we had better act accordingly.

The J-Curve Concept

Exponential growth relates to the doubling time of a quantity, whether it be interest on your money at the bank or the amount of pollution generated in a given country.

In principle it is the same as this proposal: I will work for you for thirty days. All you have to pay me is a penny the first day and then double it each day thereafter. I would earn one cent the first day, two cents the second, four cents the third, eight cents the fourth, sixteen cents the fifth. Doubling steadily, by the tenth day it has reached $5.12. Modest, perhaps, but already alarming. By the fourteenth day, the work will cost $81.92. On the eighteenth day, it will be $1,310.72; by the twenty-second, $20,971.52; and on the twenty-fifth day, $167,772.16.

The thirtieth day will climax with wages of $5,368,709.12 for that day alone. From one penny to more than five million dollars in one month!

Population also grows exponentially, and this fact is central to all our major ecological concerns. World population, like those penny wages, grew very slowly for a long time. But now, like those same wages multiplied, population is sky-rocketing. This brings us to the crucial concept of exponential growth, that of the J-curve.

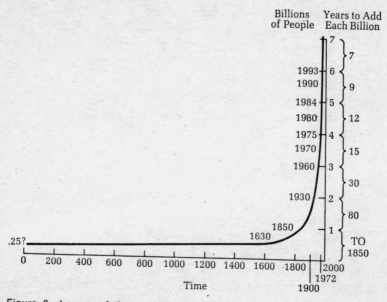

Figure 3. J-curve of the world's population, past and projected (based on present trend of growth)

Figure 3 depicts a J-curve. It could just as easily be a J-curve depicting graphically how the penny wages grew in the example given, although it actually refers to world population. In this, as in any other J-curve, things happened slowly for a long while. Steadily the world population grew until there were one billion people in the year 1850. Eighty years later, by 1930, population had doubled. Suddenly there were *two* billion. With this same trend continuing, the population will again have doubled by 1975, only forty-five years later, with four billion people. In 125 years, a brief moment in time, we will have quadrupled.

Examining the curve in Figure 3, it can be seen that we have rounded the elbowlike curve on the J and now, abruptly, we are shooting straight up. Count 1975 as our present point on the J-curve. We are now in the midst of a wild population ride skyward, unless something is done. The world population is not only growing exponentially; its doubling time is becoming shorter. Assuming present trends continue, we will have eight billion people on our planet by the year 2010, just thirty-five years from 1975. Thirty years after that, 2040, the global total will be *sixteen* billion—four times the present population.

Within the lifetime of a baby born today.

In the United States our birth rate has slowed, but we are still growing. In 1973 there was a birth every 9.5 seconds; a death every 16 seconds. As long as births exceed deaths, we will continue to grow.

On a global scale, births are exceeding deaths by 200,000 per day—or 70 million a year. The larger portion of this world population growth comes from lesser-developed areas. Because birth rates tend to fall as a nation develops, the pattern could change in the years ahead. One stumbling block to optimism, though, is the fact that close to 40 percent of our planet's people today are under fifteen years of age: a huge future breeding population.

This is the population bomb of which Paul Ehrlich and others speak, and about which we have been warned. As population rises exponentially, so do energy needs, depletion of nonrenewable resources, and every kind of pollution. The world's electric power capacity, for example, is now growing at the rate of 8 percent a year, doubling every 8.7 years. The same is true in most other areas of our lives; only the specific

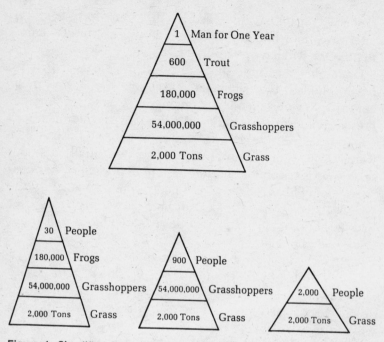

Figure 4. Simplified food chains, showing effects of eating lower on the food chain

statistics change. The formula is simple: the more people there are, the more food, housing, energy and everything else they consume. This intimately affects every aspect of our lives. "Future shock," of which Alvin Toffler wrote, is a direct result of exponential growth.

Everyone in the world does not consume at the same level. Naturally, those who have less consume less; those who have more consume more. It follows that those who consume the most will have the most profound impact on the total environment. That's getting close to home. It means us—the most consumption-minded people the world has ever seen.

A simplified food chain will help to show what we are talking about.

All animal life, including man, can trace its nourishment back to plant life. If an animal is a meat-eater, it feeds on animals that thrive on plants. Figure 4 illustrates this type of food chain. Here we can see that 2,000 tons of grass would feed 54,000,000 grasshoppers, which in turn would supply 18,000 frogs, which would take care of 600 trout, which would feed one man for one year.

One person.

Now let's see what would happen if man ate lower on the food chain. If instead of devouring trout he ate frogs, thirty people could be kept alive for a year. That's still supporting only thirty people for one year. If we go one step further down the same basic food chain, 900 people could be sustained on the 54,000,000 grasshoppers, a thirtyfold increase. This is not as wild as it may seem; in many parts of the world, the grasshopper is a real delicacy.

We are now one step away from the original source, grass. What would happen if people actually sought to live directly and solely by eating grass (or perhaps its equivalent in grain)?

Two thousand people. It would take about a ton of grass a year per person.

We are not urging that you rush out and start munching grass or become a vegetarian. But there is an obvious lesson. As the food chain pyramids upward, there is more waste and heat loss at each point of recycling. This becomes more relevant when we consider the resources it takes to produce beef steaks, roasts and hamburgers; 60 percent of our protein comes from meat, while much of the world lives on a diet of only 3 percent meat. Every year dogs in this country consume enough protein to feed four million human beings.

In frontier times, with fewer people and seemingly unlimited wildlife, everyone could eat meat without noticing any depletion. But as population soars, the situation is much changed. When a society becomes as affluent and urban-oriented as that of the United States, the demands on the environment increase exponentially. The problems of ecology tie in directly with consumption. This is the reason it is the middle class that is putting the gravest strain on the environment—not the poor.

"The poor produce less than one-third of the babies born each year [in America] and less than 20 percent of the babies are nonwhite," ecologist G. Tyler Miller, Jr., reminds us. We have to place the responsibility for superconsumption squarely where it belongs—on the middle-class American. We are using more and more energy. We are eating off the top of the food chain. If everyone tried to eat as the average American does, estimates Miller, probably two-thirds of the people in the world would die. There just isn't enough food from the top of the chain, and no food-production miracle is about to supply it either. One American living primarily on a beef diet and driving a car will have about *fifty* times more impact on the environment than the average peasant living in India.

A poor family may have ten children without causing the impact that a middle-class American birth would. It would, of course, enormously lower that family's chances of ever rising from its poverty. The fewer children in a family, the better opportunity each child has to improve his economic status in the future.

But what we have to take into consideration is that the underdeveloped peoples of the world are striving to attain our North American standard of living. If these peoples do become heavier consumers and their populations continue to rise, our planet's life-sustaining systems will be sorely challenged.

As science writer Isaac Asimov has put it, "There is a race in man's future between a death-rate rise and a birth-rate decline and by 2000, if the latter doesn't win, the former will."

The Club of Rome Projections

The Club of Rome is an informal association of about seventy scientists, educators, economists, humanists, industrialists and civil servants from twenty-five countries. Many are Nobel Prize laureates; none holds public office. Formed in 1968 in Rome, the group is dedicated to assessing mankind's most pressing problems and to seeking practical solutions.

Feeding exquisitely complex data into computers, technicians projected present-day trends in world population, industrialization, pollution, food production and resource depletion a century or more into the future. They eventually arrived at three conclusions:

1. The world will reach its limits to growth within the next hundred years. If the world continues to that level, a sudden, uncontrolled extinction of people will follow (at least five *billion*) and the world's industrial system will collapse. How will this extinction occur? It could be from famine, epidemics, pollution or war.

2. We can avoid this world catastrophe if we take serious action to halt the present growth trends and to produce economic and environmental stability. To do this we must satisfy every person's basic needs and offer him an opportunity to attain his human potential.

3. The sooner we start working toward global stability, the better our chances are of achieving it. If no planning is done, man may be a doomed species.

Working on the assumption that all the present trends will persist, the Club of Rome computers predicted a number of crises within the next few decades. A desperate land short-age will occur before the year 2000; symptoms will appear long before the crisis itself, in the form of exceedingly steep food prices, for one thing. Fresh water will become critically limited. Nonrenewable resources such as silver, tin, uranium, petroleum, natural gas and copper will increasingly be de-pleted, thereby making them inordinately costly by the end of another century. Pollution, now rising exponentially and much of it faster than population, could lead to a gigantic disaster; we can easily pass the danger point without realiz-ing it until later. Even if pollution ceased this instant, it would take many, many years for its evidence to fade from the environment.

These projections are based on all trends continuing *as they are now*—in other words, if we go blindly on, heedless of the warnings we've already had.

Does this leave any room for optimism? Certainly; quite a lot—if we, the inhabitants of this troubled planet, are will-ing to change. In fact, we just could end up with a better world than we have today! It depends on us.

The Club of Rome computers were first programmed to look for "easy" ways out of the oncoming crisis. But patch-ing-up approaches were proved to be inadequate; each one only delayed the five billion deaths. Desalinization of ocean water won't solve our water problems—where does the left-over salt go? Nuclear energy may produce more of a problem than a solution. Geophysicist M. King Hubbert has termed nuclear wastes "a perpetual hazard" that could threaten us for five hundred years. Increasing world food production, as demonstrated by the Green Revolution, tends to worsen eco-nomic inequality by driving poor farm laborers into cities, where, unemployed, they cannot buy the extra food that is produced.

In the end, there was no way to prevent the projected extinction without taking steps that may seem drastic to most of us. Here is what the Club of Rome came up with—a formula which allows for a stable quality of life within the context of a world population of about four billion:

Population must be stabilized by setting the birth rate equal to the death rate in 1975. This will amount to a 30 percent reduction in the birth rate. Industrial capital may increase *slightly* until 1990; then it, too, must be stabilized.

Beginning in 1975, we must cut to *one-fourth* the resources we use (based on 1970 values), and pollution must be reduced to one-fourth. In other words, cuts by 75 percent. At the same time, we must begin moving toward a new emphasis in several economic and social areas. We (all the world) must ensure that there be sufficient food for *all* people; hunger leads to instability in the world system. To this end, the soil must be made richer and urban organic wastes will have to be composted and recycled. From now on, what we build must last; we can't afford the wasteful obsolescence of our past. In the process of making these changes, we must move away from the consumption of factory-produced material objects and toward the "consumption" of social services—such as education—that will improve the individual without depleting our severely limited natural resources.

Once the world has been stabilized in this fashion, it probably would be a much better one than we now have. Each earthling's services would be tripled, his food doubled. (Today millions all over the world are malnourished and many are starving.) Worldwide average income, though less than today's in the United States, would be tripled. If the United States exchanged its current fertility rates for zero population growth, there would be one thousand dollars a year more in per capita income than at present. The logic is that of simple, incontestable mathematics: the smaller the family, the more each member of it has.

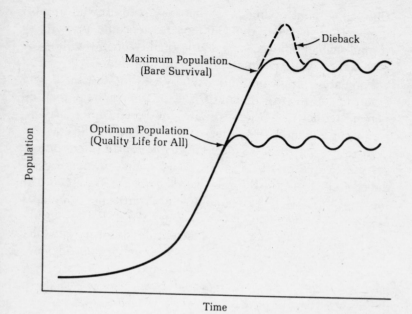

Figure 5. Two levels of population. One involves bare survival for all and
the other involves the opportunity for a quality life for all

And with stability, which can free us from the necessity
of wrestling with problems of growth, our technology would
have time to find ways of adjusting to our depleting resources.

As Dr. Dennis L. Meadows and his Club of Rome associates with the MIT Project Team point out, "the possibilities
within an equilibrium state are almost endless." Such stability could lead to the golden age of mankind, in which we
could pursue growth inwardly, achieving our full human
potential through education, art, music, religion and science.
We could harness the sun's rays as a pollution-free energy
source and concentrate on making our planet perpetually
livable through recycling, conservation and natural pest
control.

It might not be Nirvana, but it's the only road left leading toward Nirvana, *for what we are willing to give up now will determine the kind of world we will have in the future, or indeed if we will have a world at all.*

This means, more than ever before, that if you're not doing all you can for your environment, then you're not doing all you can for your future.

An Environmental Check List

The following can be used as a daily or weekly reminder.

Computing your points for this section is optional. If you wish to do so, this check list can be used on either a weekly or a monthly basis. A minimum of 30 points is desirable. Some of the items, such as the one relating to population, can give you permanent points; others must be acquired through daily or weekly actions.

	Points
• Active involvement in two or more reliable ecological organizations related to the issues discussed in this chapter, such as the Audubon Society, the Sierra Club, the Wilderness Society, Zero Population Growth, Friends of the Earth, Common Cause or any antipollution group. Work for peace. Demand clean air and water laws. The more involved you are locally, the better	10
• If there is no local group in your particular area of concern, organize one. This gives you these points for a year	20
• Having two or fewer children (you can gain points whether you're married or not)	5
• Turning off all unneeded lights	5
• Riding a bike or walking when you're going less than one mile	5
• Taking or organizing a car pool to go to work or meetings	5
• Using the bus or other mass transit	5
• Using no disposable products	5
• Lobbying to outlaw disposable products	5
• Regularly taking waste products to the recycling center	5
• If there is no recycling center where you live, you earn these points for a year by helping to start one	10

	Points
● For every speech you make on ecology	5
● For every letter you write a politician (or every politician you see) about ecology in a given week	5
● Having your own garden, whether it's on an acre of land or in your backyard or is a few plants on your apartment window ledge	5
● If it's grown with compost, manures or other natural fertilizers, add these points	5
● Being satisfied with less than white in your washing	5
● Getting others interested and involved in the ecological struggle. For every person you recruit, give yourself these points for six months	10

If you think of other ways to improve your environment, give yourself 5 points for each thing you do.

And remember, if you can get two other persons to become involved in the improvement of our environment, and if you ask each of them to recruit two others—and on and on—you will be starting a J-curve of environmental concern.

That's the kind of exponential growth we need.

4

Nutrition—Keeping It Simple

Nutrition can be as complicated as a maze. If you start studying every available book on the subject, you will encounter intricate biochemical and medical facts every few pages. Experts frequently clash, sometimes exchanging violent words. One authority insists on this, another on that. Who is right? What is one to do?

The Human Life Styling approach to nutrition can be summed up in three words: *Keep it simple.*

Accordingly, we have outlined a simple approach that is safe and can only benefit you. At the end of this chapter you will find a check list of ten prescriptions designed to cover the nutritional needs of most people. That, basically, is the nutritional program for Human Life Styling.

First, though, we will outline the predicate for that check list, by presenting a survey of certain nutritional principles that will help you understand why we think the simplified steps will improve your health.

You don't have to remember anything in this chapter but the check list at the end. Our purpose is only to explain to you, in as nontechnical language as we can, background material for the ten steps.

The important thing, after you've read this chapter, is to start *using* the check list.

The best part of it is that you won't be asked to sacrifice yourself by "dieting." Instead of "giving up" things, you will be asked to substitute. Basically you will be substituting food for nonfood. By food, we mean fresh, whole foods without poisons or other additives. It is food that is as unprocessed as possible before it reaches the dining table. On the other hand, by nonfood we mean items in our diet that do not contribute fully to our nutritional needs. They may have been overmilled or overprocessed. They may have additives. They may be relatively empty of nutritional value, except for calories. They may be performing the same function in the body as drugs do.

Among a group of Dr. McCamy's patients, especially older ones first reporting in, he found that as much as 80 percent of their diets consisted of nonfood. All we are asking in this chapter is that you eat food, in order to do for your body what is natural and normal.

Simple? Yes. Easy? Not necessarily. For many, it may involve a radical change in life style.

You do not have to change overnight. Changes can be made slowly and in their relative order of importance. This will enable you to steadily lower your risks of falling victim to almost all illnesses, while at the same time instituting the program gradually. Instead of embarking on a crash program, you will be changing your entire life style. That takes time.

If you need the security of a cliché at this stage, remember: Rome wasn't built in a day. Give yourself time to change. But see that you do change, periodically showing progress. Keep a record. Write down your personal nutritional goals after you have finished this chapter. Check yourself weekly or monthly; better yet, have someone else check your progress for you, as a doctor would. Another person can be more objective about it than you may be.

Set yourself a time schedule, aiming toward an optimal diet in, say, six months—or a year. This is more likely to work in the long run. If you can pull off a personal revolution in less time, and keep the innovations as part of your permanent life style, then fine! But for most of us it is more effective to hew away slowly at a new regimen, modifying our life habits one at a time.

The proof of nutrition's vital importance has been mounting steadily, decade after decade. Each week brings new medical evidence. But no research has yet surpassed Dr. Weston A. Price's monumental international study of nutrition's role in health. A medical anthropologist, Dr. Price spared no expense or effort in locating his human subjects, from the Eskimos of the frozen north to the Alpine Swiss to the natives of equatorial Africa. Everywhere he went, he compared the health of the primitive inhabitants with that of people living on a modernized, refined diet. In most instances he was able to find subjects of the same racial strain living under different dietary circumstances. In every case, those eating their traditional or native diet were well, while those subsisting on refined modern foods were degenerating. Since Dr. Price was a dentist, he was especially interested in matters related to his profession: cavities, dental arch and facial formation. Soon a rule of thumb developed: store-bought food paved the way for store-bought teeth. Dr. Price was able also to relate dental health to total body health. Where caries were rampant, for example, giving birth was more difficult. Dental caries constituted the earliest sign of physical degeneration.

As merely one demonstration of Dr. Price's findings, we

can see what a difference nutrition has made in the photographs that Dr. Price took of two groups of native Maoris in New Zealand. In Figure 6 Maori individuals are eating a traditional diet. They enjoy beautifully formed teeth, with wide dental arches, and are free from caries. In their primitive state, the Maoris had only about one tooth per thousand teeth attacked by decay. But in Figure 7 we see the effects of the white man's white food on these magnificent people. Tooth decay has become prevalent. The Maoris in Figure 7 are on refined, modernized diets, and their bodies are paying the penalty in, among other things, abscessed teeth and cavities.

Over and over, Dr. Price showed that the native whole foods kept the individual resistant to disease and degeneration. The particular foods varied from one geographical location to the next, yet the native diets were sufficient. The people remained strong and healthy—until they were exposed to refined foods. In Swiss valleys he found people living zestfully on milk, cheese and cereals. These were whole foods that produced whole persons. But in some of the villages refined foods had taken hold, spreading dental caries and illnesses.

The pattern continued wherever he went. Among the isolated Gaelics of the Outer Hebrides Islands, there was no milk but the people were healthy and well-formed; they ate fish. He described one Eskimo woman, married to a white man, who had had twenty children. She ate native food, including dried and smoked salmon; she had *not one cavity*. But when eight of her family went over to modern foods, 41 percent of their teeth were decayed.

Price talked with doctors in these regions. One who had been with Alaska's Eskimos and Indians for thirty-six years had never seen a case of malignant disease among the truly primitive. But when these same people became modernized, malignancies proliferated. The same findings were reported for arthritis, tuberculosis and other states of physical degeneration.

Throughout, he found the worst of the white man's diet to be white flour, jams and jellies, canned vegetables and sugar. Under whatever guise the white man had come, he had left his flawed food habits. In Melanesia, missionaries had encouraged the people to adopt the habits of modern civilization. There, Price found, toothache caused by abscessed teeth was the only cause of suicide.

Wherever Price went—Australia, Peru, Polynesia, Africa—he found the same results. The more modernized the diet, the worse the health. At each place, he examined the people he met and photographed them. Their teeth repeated the same astounding story. In their native states, these people seemed to have found the means of disease prevention. Their natural life styles ensured their resistance. The comparison in life styles is startling and should be enough to persuade the staunchest cynic of the efficacy of the natural way of living. Yet urban modern man has paid relatively little attention. Perhaps we have been too smug or too proud. An encounter Price had with an Indian in the Canadian Northwest is revealing. Price found the Indians there did not get scurvy, but white men did. (The Indians ate the adrenals and other organs of the moose, which were high in vitamin C.)

"When asked why he did not tell the white man how [to avoid scurvy]," Price wrote, "his reply was that the white man knew too much to ask the Indian anything."

Today, with our peoples' health deteriorating, we cannot afford such wasteful pride. "Uncivilized" peoples of the world, past and present, can teach us much.

Although the primitives of the world are decreasing because of the encroachments of civilization, there are still enough of them today to confirm Price's findings of several

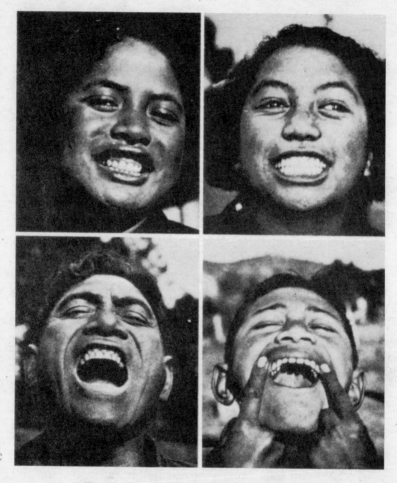

Figure 6. Maori natives eating a traditional diet

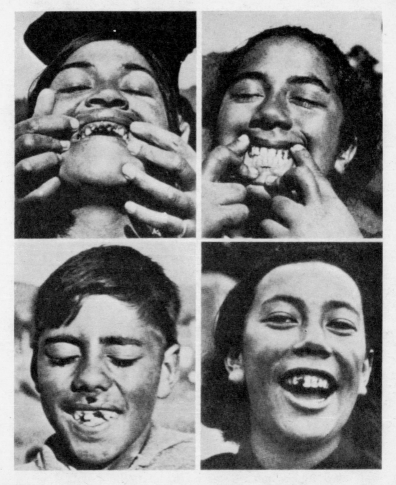

Figure 7. Maori natives eating a refined, modern diet

years ago. When Dr. McCamy was in Alaska about a dozen years ago, the Eskimos in Saint Lawrence and Adak islands were still relatively healthy. They hadn't been in much contact with our so-called civilization. This was particularly true of the older persons; they had beautiful mandibles, with not a cavity in their heads, good lung capacity, and they lived to a rather advanced age.

Now, this is highly significant, for we can't compare the life span of an Eskimo with that of a person in the temperate zone. The constant cold doubles, possibly triples, the stress on the Eskimo's body. It is questionable whether anyone ever adapts fully to such freezing temperatures. Yet there were some very old, and healthy, people there.

Dr. McCamy found the same evidence Price had reported. These Eskimos ate no refined foods whatsoever. Their diet, however, was very high in fats, but it was whale fat, fish oil and fish—all of it far more unsaturated than the beef diet on which so many Americans exist. In the summer they have rose hips, which contain high quantities of vitamin C. They were very active, even in winter, and their stress level was probably lower than he had ever seen in any primitive, or natural, society. They were mostly trim people. The only fat Eskimos were those in mainland Alaska who were working on construction jobs—and eating large quantities of candy. It's amazing how easily so-called natural tribes can get hooked on sugar when civilization beckons them. Then all of a sudden they begin suffering from colds, measles and tuberculosis, and lose their teeth at a very early age.

Dr. McCamy saw the same thing happen in Honduras several years ago when he served as a medical volunteer in hurricane relief. The Indians who were living inland on a natural diet did have parasites, but they were a slim-bellied, strong, muscular, active people with a full complement of healthy teeth. As they began to move to the coast and work in the shrimp factories, they also began eating bacon fat and sugar. Their coffee was half sugar, half coffee. Some of them were probably consuming the equivalent of 100 to 150 teaspoonsful of sugar a day! Those Indians were dreadfully sickly. Few children were surviving past the age of three or four, and those who did had huge swollen bellies, the universal badge of malnutrition.

As pitiful as those Honduras Indians were, we have little to be smug about in this country. Chronic disease in young people ought to be a very rare event and yet it is becoming more and more frequent. When Dr. McCamy was serving his stint as an Army doctor in Arkansas, almost 30 percent of the people he saw with high blood pressure were *young* people. Children in this country, who should be the healthiest of us all, have disturbing deficiencies. One ghetto study related below-normal IQs to inferior diets; those with good diets had normal IQs.

This is another way of saying that there is no difference between the body and the mind. One must be in balance for the other to function properly. The brain's neurons are subject to the same laws that govern all the other cells in the body. They must have the proper nutrients. An Emory University study illustrates this perfectly. Forty ghetto children of sixth-grade age were doing third-grade work. Diagnoses revealed inadequate personality, social deprivation, psychoses and hyperactivity. They were divided into two groups. Twenty were given breakfast—an egg, orange juice, whole wheat bread—and nothing else. The other twenty were brought in each morning and the researchers merely talked to them; the purpose of this extra attention for the control group was to ensure that breakfast would be the only variable.

The results were remarkable. The second group displayed some improvement strictly as the result of the personal attention shown them. But of the twenty who were fed breakfast, most of them, about 90 percent, jumped three grades in one year, so that they performed at their age level! On breakfast alone.

The lack of breakfast makes for irritability. The brain doesn't have adequate nourishment for it to operate smoothly. Millions in this country consume "instant" breakfasts that fizzle out into low blood sugar, complete with hunger pangs and weakness, around 10 A.M. Breakfasts such as these are probably worse than nothing; a glass of plain milk would be better.

A good diet is protective, an insurance policy against risks —for all ages. During pregnancy it can guard against birth defects, as demonstrated by many scientists, including biochemist Roger J. Williams, the discoverer of pantothenic acid and a leading figure in nutritional research. The drug thalidomide was a factor in many birth deformities several years ago; but those mothers who were not deficient in vitamin B_6 were spared the drug's strong side effects. Nutrition's major role never diminishes. Malnutrition in children has been related to mental retardation; experimentally it has been shown to reduce brain cells in rats.

The ideal form of earliest nutrition is breast-feeding for babies. It's the only natural way to nourish them, and it has no negative features. Human milk is normal for the human body for the first several months of life. The Senate Select Committee on Nutrition and Human Needs has called it "the most obvious solution to the problem of feeding an infant his or her daily dietary allowance."

From babyhood on, nutrition never takes a back seat. Until the end of your days every cell in your body needs nourishment, and the better you supply its requirements naturally and normally, the better you will feel, act, think and be.

Human Life Styling doesn't promise that you will live forever or even 120 years or more, like a Hunzakut. After all, you have to take into consideration the susceptibility factors you have accrued in years past. But there's nothing you can do about what is done, so why fret over it? You can do something about improving your health for the future. The longer your cells are provided with the necessities of life, which must include full nutrition, the longer they'll continue to remain in good working order.

For the next several pages we will be examining specific elements of nutrition in terms of resistance and susceptibility, as a prelude to the nutritional recommendations. We do not claim this is the definitive word on nutrition; instead we have attempted to classify the various facets in order of their relative importance.

We will begin with refined carbohydrates, which Dr. Weston A. Price has labeled "the white plague." Refined carbohydrates consist of sugar and white starch products. These overrefined nonfoods may be the leading cause of disease in this country today. Think back to early primitive man and his diet. Whatever he ate, we can be certain of one thing: he had no refined carbohydrates. Of these, sugar is the most pervasive.

Sugar

Sugar is a true susceptibility factor. It has no redeemable nutritional value; it is a pure carbohydrate devoid of other dietary factors. In plain words, it contributes calories—nothing else.

There are six major reasons why sugar should not be eaten. They apply to all refined carbohydrates, but especially to sugar because of its high concentration.

1. *Sugar, being a refined substance, is like a drug; it is absorbed too rapidly into the system.* Our bodies were never

meant to have such a staggering load of sucrose as you find in a cola, a ginger ale, ice cream or a piece of cake. Almost as soon as it hits the digestive tract, *whoosh!* it goes straight into the bloodstream. If it's drunk, it goes in faster than if it's in a solid form. This creates a sudden demand on the pancreas to supply insulin to control the sugar, possibly a hundred times more than the insulin output should be for such a brief period of time. There suddenly is more glucose than the body needs.

2. *This brutal overload of sugar upsets the entire endocrine balance.* The endocrine system of the body consists of the ductless glands such as the pancreas, adrenals and pituitary. These are all interrelated. High insulin levels can depress thyroid and pituitary function. It may be a factor in early menopause. As the dumped sugar throws one gland out of kilter, the others become unbalanced. Eventually malfunctioning endocrine glands may affect the brain and, therefore, all other parts of the body.

3. *Sugar is deceptive because of its concentration, and this leads to overconsumption.* British researchers T. L. Cleave and G. D. Campbell have labeled this as perhaps its leading danger. Citing the five-ounce-a-day average per person that is consumed in Great Britain, they emphasize that a person would have to eat two and a half pounds of sugar beet to supply that much sugar. Who would eat so many sugar beets every day? The concentrated nature of sugar leads readily to overconsumption. Cleave and Campbell build a convincing case that overconsumption of sugar (and refined starches) can lead to diabetes, obesity and coronary thrombosis. Dr. John Yudkin, another distinguished British scientist, thinks that in addition to these diseases, sugar may also be a factor in cancer, eye disorders, accelerated aging and other medical problems.

4. *Because it is overrefined, sugar is an incomplete carbo-*

hydrate. It has none of the protein and other food factors that accompany it in a natural food. This means sugar lacks the nutrients that are needed to metabolize it. If these nutrients aren't with the sugar at the time, they must come from the body's reserves. Thus, sugar may rob the body of vitamins B_1 (thiamine) and B_2 (riboflavin), niacin, vitamin B_6 (pyridoxine), magnesium, cobalt and other factors. Or, if the sugar doesn't metabolize completely, the body is left with waste products like lactic acid and pyruvic acid, which can become a factor in the degeneration of all the tissues and may lead to the development of arteriosclerosis.

5. *Sugar is an empty calorie.* It contributes nothing of value to the diet. Zero. Actually it is worse than zero—a minus. You do not need it at all. It leads to obesity. An empty calorie is a sick calorie. It keeps you from eating food that is valuable. Good, whole food has all the nutritional factors in the proper combinations and provides the necessary calories, too. No soft drink, for instance, has any food value at all. Why waste money and health on empty calories?

6. *The fiber has been removed from sugar.* Through the process of evolution, man in his natural state was accustomed to digesting foods with the fiber intact. His digestive tract requires coarse foods. The druglike sugar, lacking fiber, becomes the highly unnatural substance that figures in the five preceding objections. Its lack of fiber also figures in its role as a cause of tooth decay and gum disease. Children who are on high-sugar diets get tooth decay; those who eat large quantities of sugar cane (with fiber intact) do not have cavities.

In this country we consume an average of 120 pounds of sugar per person per year—adult and child. Many eat as much as 400 pounds per year. That's a national glut of sugar. (In 1900 the average was less than four pounds per year per person.) It causes no end of medical problems. Two ways it can affect health relate to its impact on blood sugar levels. It may overtrigger the insulin mechanism and cause hypoglycemia, or low blood sugar; or over a long period, perhaps twenty years, it finally breaks down the insulin-producing system, resulting in diabetes. Hypoglycemia is a major stress factor today. But since there are no lesions to be studied with a microscope, most doctors do not recognize it. Many doctors still advise patients to eat more sugar for hypoglycemia. This only starts the process over, as insulin over-reacts. The patient has a ten-minute sugar high, followed by two miserable hours of fatigue.

Yudkin and others have related sugar consumption to coronary heart disease, demonstrating that it, rather than fat, is the primary villain. Sugar has been shown to raise the cholesterol and other lipid (fat) levels in the bloodstream. The study of Yemenite immigrants to Israel is merely one example out of many. In Yemen these people used hardly any sugar at all; when they first arrived in Israel they had little incidence of heart attack, arteriosclerosis or diabetes. After they had been in Israel for several years, however, and had greatly increased their consumption of sugar, the immigrants' statistics in all three of these diseases soared alarmingly.

The old home economics view that desserts every day make for balanced meals is absolutely wrong. Work done by the Southern Academy of Clinical Nutrition has placed refined sugar at the top of the list in relation to illness. It has no redeemable nutritional value.

Old-line nutritionists are sometimes caught in the trap of believing there is no difference between one carbohydrate and another. Asked "Do you think there's a difference between eating 100 grams of baked potato and 100 grams of a cola drink—they're both carbohydrates, right?" they may reply, "Yes, they do the same thing," being unaware not only of the absorption rates of the two but of differences in their nutrients. To give you some idea of the very complicated

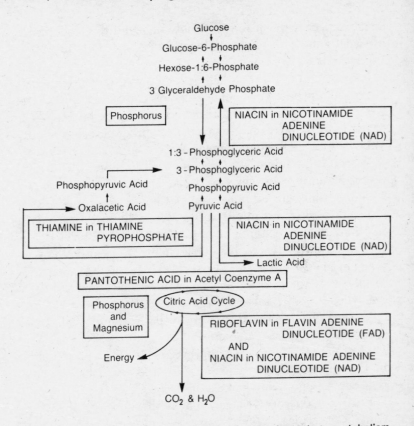

Figure 8. Points of action of the B complex in carbohydrate metabolism

process that goes on in the body during digestion, note the chemical reactions that take place, as shown in Figure 8. The body must have the necessary nutrients for metabolism. The whole potato has it, the cola does not. Just remember that digestion is a highly complex process by which cells change food into energy, requiring a complete supply of nutrients. Cofactors such as B vitamins, magnesium and cobalt are necessary at many points in the cellular cycle.

Many people have been aware of the dangers of white

sugar for years, yet it is still widely believed that some form of sweetening is necessary. This view goes against the evolutionary history of man. You should shun not only white sugar, but also brown and light brown sugar. This includes every food product in which sugar is added, whether it be pastries, canned fruit, cookies, soda pop, packaged cereals or candy in its many forms. Sugar in these products is too rapidly absorbed for the human being to handle safely.

What about honey as sweetener? Undoubtedly it is far better than refined sugar, but it, too, is a concentrated sweet. The only time natural man ever had honey was on *very* rare occasions, when he might rob a beehive. Beekeeping is a relatively late development in man's cultural history. Primitive man probably ate honey no more frequently than he drank fermented or distilled liquors. By justifying sugar or a lot of honey to yourself, you open the door of logic to daily heavy loads of alcohol for all age levels.

We even have biblical support in the warning of Solomon: "It is not good to eat much honey."

Most people's symptoms improve merely through the eliminating of sugar from their diets. Frequently just three days without it is enough to make a difference.

But what do you replace sugar with? Food—fresh, whole fruits like apples, grapes, bananas and papaya. Fruit contains sugar, too, but in a natural state with all the factors needed to make it a healthy part of you.

White Starches

Other refined carbohydrates fall into the same category as sugar. The reason sugar is worse is that it is eight times more refined than white starch. That makes it eight times worse. But this does not lessen white starch's role in disease as a susceptibility factor. White flour, white bread and "snack foods" have been overmilled. Whole-grain fractions have been taken away to increase storage life—and profit. The results are white rice, white spaghetti, white macaroni, white soda crackers, potato chips and any other kind of starch that man has tampered with.

Classifying sugar and white starch together in their effects on the body, British scientists Cleave and Campbell have blamed these refined carbohydrates for causing one disease that takes many forms, including coronary thrombosis, diabetes, peptic ulcer and hemorrhoids. Briefly, their argument about peptic ulcer is that protein is a buffering agent for hydrochloric acid, which attacks the stomach lining. When carbohydrates are refined, the protein is removed totally or almost so. Fats, starches and sugars do not affect the acid; only protein does. With fiber removed from these products, they are chewed less, and thus less alkaline saliva accompanies them to the stomach. The acid that forms in the stomach is enhanced by the absence of natural buffering processes. After years of such a diet, an ulcer appears.

Ironically, ulcer patients are usually advised to avoid coarse foods, when it is the absence of coarse foods that caused the condition. Frequent feedings of refined foods are encouraged—though it is the loading of the stomach that causes hydrochloric acid to reappear. Cleave and Campbell advise, on the contrary, feeding of unrefined food only when hungry, a profound but logical departure from present-day practices.

What injures stomach membranes, insist Cleave and Campbell, is not coarse food but unbuffered hydrochloric acid.

They go on to explain how white starches cause varicose veins and hemorrhoids. First white starches, having lost their fiber in milling, lead to constipation as they fail to provide the bulk necessary to push waste through the bowels. The constipated mass in the colon exerts pressure on the arteries and veins at the back of the abdomen. This unnatural stress creates abnormalities that eventually become varicose veins or hemorrhoids. Coarser foods, such as unprocessed bran, on the other hand, keep the waste pushing through the bowels with regularity, thereby preventing constipation and its associated disorders. A comparison of American Negroes and tribal Africans, both of relatively similar racial stock, indicates that colon problems are common among American blacks, but rare with Africans; it is another instance of refined versus unrefined diets.

The solution to these problems is simple. It is no sacrifice to give up tasteless white dough. It is a pleasure for the palate to substitute whole, natural carbohydrates. Take a fresh potato. Bake or lightly boil or steam it, and eat the skin, too—that's the way to maximize its nutritional benefits. But if you peel it, overcook it and then mash it before consuming it, you might as well eat the plate instead.

A good way to change over from sugar and white starch is to gather the family in the kitchen and let them help you throw out all the junk: the candy, cookies, chocolate-coated "goodies," white bread, Danish pastries, fruit drinks (not fresh juices) and white crackers. Bring in whole-grain breads, fresh fruit juices, wheat germ, unprocessed bran and whole-grain cereals. Learn to make bread. Substitute fresh meals for TV dinners. The older children may be disgruntled for a while, but remember this is an entire life style change. They may become the leaders. It is important that the whole family participate. You can't program your children to avoid junk if you eat it yourself.

Additives and Poisons

The average American eats from the storage shelf and in quick-food stands, where many foods, such as ice cream, may have scores of additives to soften, color and flavor. Delicatessen foods such as bologna and frankfurters contain nitrates, which have been classified as leading factors in colonic cancer.

Ideally, if you can do it, replace chemically preserved foodstuffs with food you grow yourself or buy from a farmer who uses no additives or sprays on his crops. Organic gardening is done without the use of commercial fertilizers and pesticides. If you can't do this, try to buy from a fresh fruit and vegetable stand. Check labels on everything you buy. Reject those that list among the ingredients BHA, BHT, artificial flavoring, artificial coloring, or other such terms that indicate petroleum derivatives and other chemical additives. Consider them as poisons.

Another way to cut out or cut down on additives is to eat lower on the food chain, which helps prevent the impact of the concentrating effects of pesticides. Swordfish, at the top of a long food chain, ends up with more mercury. The fat in meat has more DDT than vegetables. Discarding the fat in meat will help eliminate DDT and other such poisons.

In the coming years we must start growing our plants and nourishing our animals the organic way. The purely selfish desire of survival dictates it for the human race.

Smoking

Smoking is included in this chapter on nutrition in order to simplify the program. Almost everyone knows the dangers of smoking by now. The Surgeon General long ago made it official. It is more than a matter of nicotine and tars. Smoking brings a very high heat into the sensitive tissues of the respiratory system. Furthermore, since growing tobacco plants are drenched with pesticides, the smoker is exposed to those poisons also.

The dangers of smoking aren't restricted to the smoker.

Nonsmokers in the same room with a smoker are forced to breathe in the noxious gases caused by combustion processes, which may be more deadly than the original smoke sucked in by the smoker himself.

Smoking is completely incompatible with health. Along with the risks of cancer, bronchitis and emphysema, smoking depletes the body of its nutrients. It blocks oxygen transfer from the lungs into the blood, leading to imbalances in electrolytes and blood gas. There may be other losses, of which we aren't aware.

Dr. McCamy has found in his practice that most people will stop if the risks are clearly stated and the patient is advised (as we now advise you, as of this moment), "You *must* stop smoking for any level of acceptable health."

It is difficult to stop smoking. If you try cutting down, you might change at first to a pack a day of one of the filter-tip cigarettes, which taste so bad you'll wonder why you smoked in the first place. That could induce a positive attitude. Then after a month on a low tar cigarette you'll need to stop completely. Tapering down almost never works; too often people return to smoking too much. Nicotine tablets only help take away the slight nicotine effect, without reducing the need for doing something with your hands. Whatever you do, a period of nervousness can be expected until you get it under control.

Whenever possible, substitute. Carry twenty carrot or celery sticks in your pocket, and every time you want a cigarette take out a carrot stick and mouth it as you would a cigarette. It may sound silly, but try it. Just don't substitute foods that might be fattening.

Or take a brisk, brief walk instead of a cigarette. If you're at the office, take three slow, long, deep breaths, then walk to the water cooler and back. That's your cigarette. You may do this a hundred times the first day. A lot of walking and a lot of carrots, but after two or three weeks it'll drop down to ten or twenty times a day or much less. The carrots won't make you fatter, the walking will help you, and few people breathe deeply enough anyway. Think of it as substitution: *I'm going to do this instead of smoking. I'm doing something for my lungs. I'm improving the health of my mouth. I'm keeping my hands occupied. I'm helping my mind function better.*

The craving for a smoke may not be completely absent for years. This depends on the individual. If the problem is greater than you feel you can handle by yourself, seek out Smoke Watchers or any such group that may be available locally.

The entire Human Life Styling program will help smokers get off their habit. Aerobic exercises especially prove valuable. It's hard to run, walk or ride a bike if you're smoking. Exercise dramatizes the handicap; hard breathing makes you realize what has been happening to your lungs. We have found that the average smoker, after being on the total program for six months, just didn't want to smoke anymore.

Saturated Fats

There is almost no need in the human diet for saturated fats. In this nation we use tons of saturated fats in the form of chili, fried foods, hamburgers and hydrogenated foods.

When the cholesterol scare first came up about a decade ago, margarines became all the rage. That's great, we thought. It's better than butter and it will lower cholesterol! What we didn't know at the time is that the process starts with perfectly good corn or soy oil, which then is hydrogenated. Hydrogenation means that the hydrogen bonds in the fat are welded, producing a hard fat that is solid at room temperature—a saturated fat. It is harder than butter.

Since hydrogenated fats are the hardest and worst of all, they should be avoided wherever they appear in commercial margarine, peanut butter, mayonnaise or any other food. If you use these foods, make certain that the label confirms that they are unhydrogenated; usually you have to buy them at health food stores.

Beef fat is very hard at room temperature, while chicken and fish fat are markedly softer. Safflower and vegetable oils, on the other hand, are liquid at room temperature; they are unsaturated.

You need fat in your diet. The Southern Academy of Clinical Nutrition has proved that we need fat to live. It is a resistance factor. But we need more unsaturated fat. We need "fresh" fat, not the burnt or used kind one finds in short-order stands that deep-fry fish, chicken and potatoes. Avoid eating anything fried. The heating of fats, including unsaturated fats, in frying produces carcinogens.

Ideally you would use only "fresh," unsaturated fat such as that in safflower oil, soy oil, saffron oil or corn oil, and these in salads rather than in cooking. Avoid *all* hydrogenated foods. If you're a heavy beef eater, alternate your beef meals with chicken and fish. Diet is recognized as basic to any treatment of high blood fats; all drugs for lowering cholesterol or triglycerides have some side effects. If you can't get unhydrogenated, unsaturated fats at your grocery store, demand it even if you have to scream at them. Or go to a health food store.

Inevitably the question arises as to whether or not to use whole milk. If you can obtain certified raw milk and it seems appropriate to drink it, go ahead. You might note, however, that about 30 percent of the population is allergic to milk to some degree and many people drink too much of it. If you have bowel problems, you might consider doing without milk, to see if that helps. There is a controversy in nutritional circles over milk. Dr. Melvin E. Page thinks no milk at all should be allowed in the diet; Adelle Davis recommends a high milk diet of around two quarts a day. We stand somewhere between these views. Whole milk contains saturated fat, but up to a glass a day of raw milk or some cheese may be acceptable if you have no adverse reaction.

Drugs

To simplify, we have classified as drugs: alcohol, coffee, tea and other caffeinated drinks, marijuana, sleeping pills, LSD, tranquilizers, diuretics or water pills, diet pills, "speed," aspirin and pain killers. All of these tamper with the body in some way and provide no nourishment. Any drug may have a side effect, ranging from suppression of the appetite to robbing the body of vital nutrients. The average American takes from three to five such mind-and-body altering drugs a day. Unless there's an urgent medical reason, it's best to shun them all.

Except in the case of very high blood pressure, the simple practice of restricting salt, increasing potassium and taking vitamin B_6 will eliminate the need for diuretics. Dr. John M. Ellis has proved that vitamin B_6 alone will relieve edema, or water retention, in most instances.

We consider it illogical to use diet pills. An appetite suppressant makes for an inbalance in the hypothalamic hunger mechanism, the weight-control mechanism and the bodily mechanisms regulating depression and awareness. When the pill is withdrawn, the person may become even hungrier and thus gain more weight. If you are taking diet pills you have two choices: stop taking them or become dependent on them for the rest of your years. It is of course better never to take them at all. The way to lose weight is to methodically change your life style—for life. As you get more in tune with the rhythms of nature, you will not need drugs.

Alcohol, like sugar, is an unnecessary caloric. Ideally, no

empty calories should be taken in. Different people handle alcohol in different ways. If you are in absolutely impeccable health, then it might be acceptable for you to have one drink a day, as long as it is not mixed with a soft drink or sugared liquid.

Coffee is an addictive drug. If you drink coffee and you don't believe this, then stop it totally tomorrow and see what headaches and depressions you will have until your body adjusts to living without it.

A high correlation with illness has been found in people who drink more than two cups of coffee a day. We've seen patients who were drinking ten, twelve, fifteen cups and wondering why they were nervous! There are probably millions of people in this country who drink more than ten cups of coffee every day. It is a susceptibility factor. Caffeine stimulates the sympathetic nervous system and the secretion of acid in the stomach; yet many patients with heartburn have never been advised to stop drinking coffee. They should have stopped at the first, tiniest sign of heartburn. Why wait until there's a bleeding ulcer?

Coffee also, for reasons not yet understood, has a fairly high ranking in the cancer profile. It could be in the processing, where sulfuric acid is used, or it could be the result of the fungi growing on the coffee beans after they have been stored too long. Or it may be the simple excess stomach acid irritation.

The high incidence of cancer correlates with heavy tea drinkers as well. Generally, what applies to coffee will fit tea also, though tea has less acid. All cola drinks and chocolate also contain caffeine.

Coffee, tea, cola and chocolate all perform the one disservice to the body that sugar does. Because they pull stored body sugar from the liver too quickly, they raise the blood sugar too high, then lower it. The best way to prevent this is to take an orange juice break in the morning instead of a coffee break. One study along these lines, conducted by Dr. McCamy, demonstrated that efficiency will go up 20 percent.

When you stop any of these caffeine drinks, you will suffer withdrawal symptoms, as you'd expect from a drug. These may include headaches, listlessness, general aches and nervousness—which gives you an insight into what this drug has been doing to you. The best way to stop is to taper down until you reach one cup a day. Hold the line there for two or three days. Then stop—or rather substitute. There are several coffee substitutes on the market, made in this country and in Europe. These, usually of grain or bran, are preferable to decaffeinated coffee, which after all has only the caffeine removed and retains some acid. Herbal teas are best of all, and there is a wide variety available. For chocolate substitute carob, which tastes better anyway. These are pluses. Decaffeinated coffee is a zero. Coffee, tea, cola and chocolate are minuses. Other aspects of the program will help you rid yourself of these crutches.

To put all drugs in their proper perspective: Don't knock the kid who's smoking "grass" if you're eating sugar and drinking coffee and booze. And the people at the church socials who condemn alcohol while eating apple pie and drinking coffee are harming their health just as much. Maybe more if they're obese, too. The effect on the disease development complex is roughly the same. They're all abnormal activities for the body.

Liquids

When the body is thirsty it needs one thing—water. People who quench their thirst with sweetened soft drinks are running a gamut of risks. By the time their thirst has been slaked, their blood sugar has been enormously raised, they have been alkalinized and they have swallowed a number of chemical additives. If thirsty, drink water.

Studies have shown that hard water is better for heart health. Many American cities today have polluted water supplies. For these reasons, spring water is preferable if you can get it, or distilled water.

Try to drink water at room temperature. Of the tribes of natural man studied for this book, none drank iced liquids. Even in the civilized world, Americans are the major consumers of iced drinks. It's abnormal for the human body. Those who drink an excess of cold liquids have more upper respiratory infections. What seems to happen is that cold liquids chill the cells in the throat and lower their resistance; the mucus supply drops immediately and bacterial invasion follows more readily.

On occasion you may wish to substitute small amounts of fresh fruit juice or vegetable juice without additives or sugar. Take the trouble to ensure that it is a genuine juice. Many juice drinks are artificial and may, like an orange drink, contain petroleum additives. Read the labels!

Protein

The literature on protein has become contradictory and confusing. Some nutritionists feel we need 80 grams of protein a day. Most people consume much less than that. Dr. McCamy has made one study indicating that upper- and middle-class women have deficient intakes. One reason for this is that foods we think of as protein are actually low in quality. Frankfurters, fat hamburgers and bologna are mainly fillers with little protein.

So the first step is to increase the quality of your protein. Eat simple foods: fresh fish, broiled; fresh baked turkey or chicken; some beef, pork or veal; eggs and some milk products. Haddock and cod are superior sources of protein. Have liver at least twice a week. Organ meats are of far higher quality protein than other cuts of meat, much better than steak and muscle meats.

Eliminate frankfurters, delicatessen meats and commercial chili. If you want to make your own stews or chili, use only fresh ingredients. Spices should be used only if you have no heartburn or bowel problems.

You will usually find that the best sources of protein are good providers of other essential nutrients as well. Eat eggs, milk, cheese, fish, chicken, beef (especially organ portions), soybeans, legumes and nuts, and you will not only ingest high-quality protein, you will also have calcium, iron, vitamin A and the B vitamins.

Some say that 80 grams of protein daily is far more than we need; others opt for a nonmeat diet. During a recent visit to Lausanne, Dr. McCamy reviewed work by Swiss and Scandinavian nutritionists that helped explain how a vegetarian could get along so well. Most of us in the United States apparently are in acid balance because of our carbohydrate and meat diets. When a person shifts his diet to more vegetables and fruit, this bodily condition changes to an alkaline balance. These Europeans' work shows that an alkaline balance ensures a much higher absorption of protein and generally better assimilation of food, and that more protein is held actively in the blood serum. The researchers found that the average person could get by on as little as 20 grams of protein daily, which is one-fourth of what some nutritionists say is necessary. We are not advocating such a change— although ecological reasons may make it necessary sometime in the future—but wish to indicate to you the range of opinions on this subject.

At the famed Bircher-Benner Klinic at Zurich, raw fruit and vegetables make up the bulk of the healthiest diet, for the sickest people. It appears that the sicker people often can't metabolize protein or fat efficiently.

Our suggestion: Improve the quality of protein and vary it by using both animal and vegetable sources together for an enhanced effect.

Meals and Freshness of Food

Americans by the millions have nothing but coffee for breakfast, grab a quick grilled lunch wolfed down with a cola drink or a beer, climaxed by a huge dinner at home. They follow up dinner with beer and potato chips and fall asleep in front of the television set. It is too much for their enzyme systems to handle at one time, and they sleep with half-digested proteins in their stomachs, a quite unhealthy practice. In the morning they are nauseated and wonder why they can't eat breakfast. Then the cycle begins again and they are tired all day.

They are not only eating the wrong things, they are putting an emphasis on the wrong meals. You need nutrients during the day when you are using energy, not after you've done your day's work. You need to take in body fuel early in the morning, so you'll have it when you need it. Most people will benefit by the policy of eating breakfast like a king, lunch like a prince and supper like a pauper. Certainly breakfast and lunch should be the larger meals.

A tossed salad and a soup can make a marvelous supper. Unless you expect to be up late, it should be sufficient. If you're in the habit of going out for dinner, why not change the routine? Go out for lunch. The same food is often served then as at dinner, and it may cost half as much earlier in the day.

For maximum utilization of your food, eat raw fruit or vegetables at every meal. The fresher food is, the better it works for you. A food grown on fertile soil, just picked, has all the enzymes and nutrients it will ever have. The longer it takes to reach your plate from the tree or vine, the more it loses in deteriorated enzymes and vitamins. This is also true of meat and fish; they have the highest food values when just slaughtered or caught.

Fruits and vegetables in some commercial markets have been stored for weeks or months before they are sold. Add to this the fact that many people go all week without eating one raw food. Such diets rank very high in cancer profiles. We need the enzymes, the roughage and all the nutrients that raw foods have—and that are usually missing in processed, canned and frozen foods.

The ideal way is to grow your own food organically, without pesticides or commercial fertilizers, and eat the food fresh, and preferably raw, as it comes from the garden. Cooling, packaging, heating, even slight heating, decrease its value. With fruit, fresh off the tree is best, from a fruit stand or from a farmer you know is next best, a market is third best, and frozen is fourth. Canned fruit should be ignored altogether. (Some diabetics, hypoglycemics and arthritics may have to restrict even some fresh fruits, like bananas, which are high in natural sugars, but for about 90 percent of us these are part of a good diet.) If you eat all fresh foods, with 50 percent raw and the rest cooked lightly or baked, you'll be making an excellent start toward better health. By using some frozen foods, while avoiding canned or packaged goods and eating nothing fried or burnt, you'll make commendable headway. At the very least, eat something fresh and raw once a day, and shun smoked or grilled foods.

The easiest way to remember this is to tie it in with your meals: Eat at least three raw foods every day.

If you have a clinical illness such as diverticulitis, you may be able to handle raw juices. Get a juicer and prepare raw juice for each meal.

If you have a tendency toward food binges, it's best to

avoid snacks completely. Eat only at meals. Chew each bite *thoroughly*. This helps make digestion more complete, as the food is broken down and mixed with saliva. Don't eat while watching television or a movie: devote full attention to your meal. If you have no problem of overweight or of overeating, legitimate snacks of real food are acceptable. Popcorn without butter or salt is not bad. Fresh vegetables or fruit is better.

A good rule of thumb is to chew each bite at least ten times. Many foods will require more chewing to make them perfectly digestible.

Start off with a bowl of homemade soup tonight for supper. In the morning you'll wake up hungry. Then begin refueling your body right—normally and naturally.

Supplements

If you lived in a mountain valley, raised your crops and all food organically, worked hard manually and had relatively no stress, you probably wouldn't need vitamin and mineral supplements. But we are living an abnormal life style in a highly urbanized civilization with a complex technology that keeps us under unrelenting stress. Our requirements must take these factors into consideration.

Air pollution, as well as smoking, increases our need for vitamin E and other nutrients. A stressful situation, in which you feel tight inside all day, may require 3,000 or even 4,000 units of vitamin C, plus larger amounts of pantothenic acid and other B vitamins, for the adrenal glands to function properly. Jet lag, or the stressful experience of crossing time belts in a brief period of time, makes additional demands on our bodies; the precise needs haven't even been learned yet.

Even if you ate well, you still would have to contend with today's poor agricultural methods, geared only to quantity production. The vitamin C in a commercially grown orange may be only one-tenth of what it was thirty years ago, because of our depleted soils. Trace minerals aren't being replaced in the soil; fertilizers only add nitrogen, potassium and phosphorus. The same is true of almost all other commercially grown agricultural products.

Diet surveys among patients have indicated that few people in this country are getting even the minimum daily requirements (MDR) of all the nutrients. That's just enough to avoid deficiency disease, the borderline beyond which you are risking a clinical disease, such as scurvy, beriberi or pellagra. Radiant health will require much more than this borderline of the MDR. A normal person who feels fantastically well may need ten times the vitamin intake of the MDR.

Dr. Weston A. Price, in his epic study of nutrition and health all over the world, found that the best primitive diets have supplied at least *four* times the minimum requirements set by modern medicine.

Everyone probably needs a general vitamin-mineral supplement, from natural sources if possible, plus a formula designed to assist our adrenal glands in coping with today's urban stress. The stress complex should contain at least 5 to 10 milligrams of vitamin B_2 and B_6, 10 to 20 milligrams of pantothenic acid, and 100 to 500 milligrams of vitamin C. If sufficient vitamin E is not present in the general vitamin, 50 to 200 milligrams of vitamin E is advisable.

Remember, however, that every one of us has specific needs. Getting a hormone analysis of the body would be ideal. Certainly everyone can benefit from a computerized dietary survey. In the appendix of this book there is a list of nutritional organizations to which you may write to obtain the names of physicians who may be able to help you with this.

Weight Control

In this country a weight-loss diet is usually looked upon as something temporary. *We recommend no temporary diets.* The only diet that's worth anything is a lifelong, methodical, permanent change of eating habits. A new life style.

If you're overweight, a good basic change is to limit your diet mainly to meats and vegetables until you've trimmed down to your ideal weight. Before that, of course, you should stop all refined carbohydrates—not one crystal of sugar, not one bite of pizza. Until you've trimmed down, you should refrain from starchy vegetables like potatoes, corn and beans. You may eat some fruit, whole-grain cereals and bread, nuts and milk products, but you must first prove to yourself that you can eat limited amounts, perhaps one of these per week, and still maintain your weight; it is best at first to avoid them completely.

Since this is a way of life and not a temporary diet, you must weigh weekly and record it, perhaps on a kitchen calendar where you will see it each day. When you reach your basic weight goal, then congratulate yourself—but don't celebrate with food. Keep recording your weight weekly. If one morning you find you've gained a pound, say from 120 to 121, go back to your basic diet of meat, liver, fish, chicken and vegetables. Not one slice of bread, not one crystal of sugar, not one taste of milk. Under no condition should anyone wishing to keep his weight down ever try sweets, white starches or fried foods again.

Some people believe it is all right to go off a diet occasionally and make up for it by more stringent eating the next day. We don't recommend it. Not everyone is psychologically geared to do so. A "caloriholic" cannot eat one piece of pie and then fast the following day unless he or she exerts an enormous amount of mental discipline. It is easier, and less strain, to do without it in the first place. This particularly applies to holidays. Overweight people have more problems at Thanksgiving and Christmas than at any other time of the year. Skip the dressing and dessert then, too.

Here are some basic pointers for losing weight. You may wish to refresh your memory, or renew your enthusiasm, by referring to them from time to time.

• Plan a lifelong weight program. Do not attempt a crash diet. It may be safer to remain heavy than to crash up and down with your weight. But realize that obesity carries high risks to your health and life.

• Get off all refined carbohydrates—sugar and white starch —*totally*. These are the villains that made you overweight.

• Maintain a basic diet of protein—meat, eggs, fish, cheese —and low-starch vegetables until you've reached your ideal weight.

• Do not substitute fats for carbohydrates. It was *refined* carbohydrates, not natural ones, that did you in.

• Maintain the basic diet for the rest of your life, but when you reach your ideal weight you can decide how much whole-grain bread, cereal and fruit you can add.

• Weigh once a week, at the same time of day. To do so immediately upon getting up, without clothes, is a good policy; this reflects a true weight.

• If your weight goes up even one pound from your ideal weight, then return to the basic diet.

• Commit yourself to eating no empty calories for the rest of your life.

• If you wish, you may divide your three meals into six snacks of the same foods each day. This facilitates weight loss.

• Never skip a meal. Remember that most fat people eat one meal a day. It lasts from 6 P.M. until midnight.

• Eat from a predetermined schedule.

• Do not eat when fatigued. This leads to overstuffing.

• Eat lightly, just what you need. Eating slowly and chewing your food carefully helps spread out the meal. It is important not to overeat, which you can do even at breakfast.

• If you chew your food until it is *creamed*, it will also help you feel full when you should.

• Never take seconds. Put what you need on your plate and limit your meal to that.

• There are no special occasions for gorging. Your heart and brain and the rest of your body have the same needs on holidays as on other days.

• When eating out, never look at the menu. Just place your order, such as steak and salad, and forget about all the other things they serve. If bread and crackers are on the table, ask the waitress to remove them; if your companion wants them, employ will power.

• Exercise before dinner. Aerobics, as described in the next chapter, is especially beneficial for busy people or harried executives who have emotional stress factors. Exercise helps tighten the stomach. It is a fallacy that exercise makes you eat more.

• The rest of the Human Life Styling program will work synergistically with your nutritional regimen, as you spiral upward in your aim toward better health.

Childhood is often where our overweight tendencies began. The way we eat has very little to do, much of the time, with what our bodies need. We eat to satisfy others, as we did in childhood to please Mother; we repeat what was fun when we were little; we satisfy frustration or neuroses; we eat to gain love, to overcome idleness and boredom, and sometimes we just spin our wheels out of habit, as when we snack during a movie. We can play some part in preventing the vicious cycle from continuing in our own children.

When a mother says, "I can stop eating sugar, but I can't keep it from my children," her logic reaches the height of absurdity. What she is actually saying is, "I'll stop poisoning myself, but I don't want to stop poisoning my children because they'll scream a bit."

Sugar and white starch contribute to obesity more than anything else in this country. Eliminate these alone from your family's diet and some weight will be lost automatically. And it should make most people better-looking. Sugar helps cause pimples. Discarding the pimple-makers and the fat-makers should make sense at any age.

Everyone has to participate in the new life style or it will create hassles. But if you have only good food in the house, there is no choice. Encourage the children to avoid candy and soft drink machines, and carry juices and vegetables and nuts with them to school.

If you want your children to be truly healthy and happy, you will have to see that the school lunches are improved. Most of these are riddled with nonfood, especially with sugar and white starch. Halloween projects present another serious problem in nearly every community. Do your part by passing out fruits and nuts at holidays.

By becoming more aware of your buying habits you can better control what is in your kitchen. Make up your list before you leave for the grocery store. Don't buy prepared snack foods. Stick to food. Eliminate nonfood.

Your Nutritional Check List (For Everyone)

If you concentrate on these ten steps, you will be able to increase the resistance factors and lower the susceptibility factors in your diet. Refer to this outline frequently as a memory refresher and to review your periodic progress.

(For those who wish to measure their progress numerically, an optional point system is provided. Strive toward a weekly or monthly total of 30 points. Set an ultimate goal of a perfect score—56 points.)

THE PROGRAM	Points
1. *No* refined carbohydrates (sugar, sweets, white starches). There is no place for these in human nutrition. They are major factors in the causation of most illnesses.	
No sugar	10
No white starch	5
2. No smoking. This has long been known to be a disease factor. You must want to stop. Carry short carrot or celery sticks or nuts as substitutes. The whole program of diet, exercise and stress reduction will help.	10
3. Alcohol is an unnecessary caloric. Drink none unless in *good* health and at your proper weight, then only one drink per day.	5
4. Use unsaturated fats. Safflower oil is best, corn oil is fair. Do not use saturated fats such as meat or bacon fat, or margarine unless it is unhydrogenated safflower margarine. *Do not fry foods.*	2
5. Eat raw fruits or vegetables at every meal. Start the meal with them. Buy foods as fresh as possible, from farmers or markets, and organically grown, if possible.	5
6. Have a large breakfast, like a king; a medium lunch, like a prince; a small supper, like a pauper. Have a protein snack at 10 A.M., 3 P.M. and 9 P.M. if you need it; toasted soybeans are excellent. The body needs nutrients when it is using them.	2
7. No coffee, tea, colas, chocolate or other caffeinated beverages. Herbal teas, decaffeinated coffee or coffee substitutes are possible alternatives.	5
8. Nutritional supplements. Most people need the minimum below. Some people may need more, even when they are eating properly. Calcium and magnesium supplements may be needed if little milk is consumed. If you take extra vitamin C, it should be spread out over the day and taken with food. It is helpful to have extra reserves of vitamin C	5

before special demands on the body, as before running exercises or before business meetings. Minimum requirements are:

(a) A general vitamin, preferably from natural sources.

(b) A stress complex formula, including equal portions of vitamin B_2 and B_6 (5 to 10 milligrams), pantothenic acid (10 to 20 milligrams) and vitamin C (100 to 500 milligrams).

(c) Vitamin E, 50 to 200 milligrams, twice a day.

9. Increase the quality of protein. Liver is best, followed by chicken, fish, beef, legumes, nuts and dairy products. Combine vegetable- and animal-source protein at meals to include all and to enhance each type. Eat no junk meats such as bologna, frankfurters or salami.

10. Drink hard spring water, if available. Use no iced drinks.

5

Descendants of Hunters

When Dr. McCamy was in medical school, he participated in a study of a Georgia county that sought to uncover the factors correlating highest with coronary heart disease.

The people of the county were surveyed as to their exercise habits, dietary patterns and incidence of heart attacks.

It was verified that bankers, whose work is almost completely sedentary, have more coronaries than laborers. If the banker walked his dog every other night, his risk remained just as high. This is to say, if one thousand bankers walk their dogs, there will be very little decrease in their coronary rate. If the banker played golf once a week, it made almost no change at all. In fact, weekend workers and weekend athletes have more coronaries. This means that if a person plays golf only once a week or works in the yard or exerts himself only on weekends, it is logical to *add on* to his percentage of risk.

Most people do not realize this, as is evident from exchanges that take place in the medical clinic. "Do you exercise?" the doctor asks the patient. "Sure," replies the patient. "What do you do?" "I bowl twice a week." This, like golf, is a good sport. You perspire a little. You swing your arms. But it does not build the heart and lung capacity needed to help the body prevent a coronary.

The same is true of the banker who golfs on weekends or walks his dog every night or so.

The Georgia study never revealed the magic point in exercise where the risk begins to drop dramatically. It was suspected, however, that two miles, walked very fast, would probably start turning the tide.

Now Dr. Kenneth H. Cooper, working with thousands of Air Force personnel, has formulated a system of exercise that does effectively shore up the heart and cardiovascular system against disease and degeneration. The system is called aerobics, and includes several types of exercises that, continued long enough each time, work through the heart and lungs to benefit the entire body. Dr. Cooper has confirmed our suspicions in the Georgia study and has gone beyond that. Aerobic exercises require hard, sustained effort and plenty of oxygen. They condition you by making you breathe harder and deeper, pump your blood better and shape up your muscles, including the heart. By studying more than fifteen thousand airmen, Cooper has arrived at a numerical measurement of the amount of aerobic exercise we need. In general terms, this is the exercise that it takes to shift to your second wind. The whole enzyme system of the body undergoes a change as a result of the increase in blood flow, muscular exertion and rapid lung respirations.

The major exercise suggestions of Human Life Styling are those of Cooper's aerobics. There is a variety of exercises to choose from, including walking, jogging and running, bike riding, running in place and swimming.

The tables at the end of this chapter were created by Cooper. One of the walking tables is for age thirty and younger. One is a progressive walking program for cardiac patients. The others are for those of age fifty or older who wish to cycle, swim, walk, run, or run in place. Anyone can use these. In fact, we have selected the age fifty tables in order to simplify and at the same time ensure complete safety for all ages. Some may find themselves performing at levels above the beginning stage; if so, you can easily adjust, as long as you don't try to go too fast too soon. The last tables are for all ages, for those who have reached a state of fitness. Six types of aerobic activities are included, as a permanent guide.

The goal of aerobic training is to build yourself up gradually to 30 points per week at whichever type of exercise you choose. The key here is *gradual*. Like all the other elements in Human Life Styling, the aim is to create a change in your life style. Just as you can't expect to modify all your nutritional habits overnight, it will take weeks and months to reach and maintain an optimal level of exercise. Then you should continue it for the rest of your life.

Our present-day human physical equipment is at least about fifty thousand years old, as far as evolutionary change is concerned. Certainly it has not changed in the past ten thousand years. You don't even have to go that far back in time to realize that the human body was used by our far-off ancestors much more than we use it in today's sedentary, motorized, industrialized society.

Primitive man, to whom we trace our ancestry, was a food gatherer and hunter. He was always on the go. When he wasn't running after wild game, he and the entire tribe were walking, moving over a wide expanse of territory to find berries, nuts, roots, fruit and edible vegetation. He didn't have horses to ride until relatively recently in his development. Only his legs could take him to where the food was.

He was active every day of his life. He had no chance to become sedentary at all until the invention of agriculture several thousand years ago—a recent event in the evolutionary development of man. With agriculture man was able to settle in one geographical location; specialization of labor followed, allowing some members of the society to work less hard than others. However, it was not until recent times, with the invention of automobiles and rapid communication, that man has become almost completely sedentary. Yet the human body has changed hardly at all during the past hundred thousand years; only our technology has, guiding our bodies toward softness.

We are the descendants of those primitive hunters and gatherers. Since we have the same body, we need to give it what those hunters and gatherers gave it regularly: exercise. It was never meant for us not to run or walk for several hours every day.

In order to enhance the value of the rest of the Human Life Styling program, aerobics is absolutely a must. We are tempted to say it is the most important part of the entire program. This change in your life style will help you get back in touch with your normal body balance.

A beginning walking program, following one of the tables, will get you going. We usually recommend that you start with thirty minutes every day, building up endurance gradually. You must measure off the distance. It's not enough to say, "Oh, I walked a half hour." The distance and your timing are both important to the overall training effect. As you step up the tempo, after a few weeks you'll be perspiring and breathing deeply. Then you are getting into it in full stride. A gentle stroll will not do the job.

Our attitudes toward exercise in this society have grown to be so abnormal that many people rebel at the thought of an aerobic regimen. "Well, that's really hard!" they may exclaim. It has to be, to make us breathe hard and sweat. In the long run it isn't as hard as watching our body machinery rust from lack of use. Others complain, "I don't have time to do it." If you don't have time for twenty or thirty minutes of exercise, then your life is too busy. It's important that you change that life.

Many of us feel that we get enough exercise during the course of the day when we actually do not. "Well, I work hard every day," we've heard many say. "I must walk ten miles during the day." Many women try to include shopping as part of their aerobic schedule. They classify, say, three hours of shopping as their exercise. All these are stop-and-start motions. It's start, stop, stand, then start again. It is like golf and bowling. It provides zero aerobic points. Even tennis is start-and-stop and hard to compile points with. It is *sustained* effort that makes the difference. The stress of standing, as you experience it in shopping, is worse than doing nothing. It's very hard on the body, for the blood tends to pool in the legs; it constitutes strain on varicosities and heart function. You still need the uninterrupted two-mile walk, or whatever aerobic activity you prefer, in addition to shopping, golfing and working.

If you're over thirty, it's advisable to have a physical examination before initiating your program. There is almost no one, however, who can't begin a walking program. Most people under forty could start walking today, aiming at covering a mile in eighteen minutes. Within sixteen *weeks*, without pushing yourself, you should be able to walk three miles in forty-two minutes or less, five days a week. As you can see, this would entail a very slow, but steady, advance in distance and decrease in time. It is recommended that you walk at least six months before starting to run, if you decide to acquire your points that way.

If you have a bicycle, you can start cycling around two miles in eleven and a half minutes, five days a week. Within sixteen weeks you should be able to have increased this to six miles in twenty-two minutes, five times a week. These are general averages for younger people.

The most important thing of all is to *do* something. Only you can do what is necessary for your body. No doctor, parent, mate, friend can do it for you. It's your responsibility altogether. Every week you should be compiling points, gradually building up until you reach 30 points a week and then maintaining it. A woman can get by with 24 points, because her risk of cardiovascular disease is less than that of a man. Cooper recommends 20 to 24 points a week for a woman; after the age of menopause, he suggests she maintain 24 points. We leave it up to the individual woman whether she achieves 24 points or, in this age of equality, works for 30 points like a man. There is no particular reason for you to accumulate more than 30 points a week unless you are training for a specific athletic event.

You do not have to do your aerobics every single day. You can skip a day. The tables will indicate for you how many days you will need to exercise. But it is best that you not skip more than one day in a row. There is a loss of aerobic benefits within forty-eight hours. This means you should walk or run or cycle or swim at least every other day. You can't skip three days, or even two, and still be in top shape. Ideally you should exercise at least five days a week without two days off in a row.

It is important to keep records of your progress. Write down what you do, so that you can look back and see how you did that week, how many points you stacked up. It's the only way to be sure you know what you've really done. Without a written record, you would be unable to compare one week's total activity with that of the preceding one. One way to keep tabs is to log up your daily total of miles or points on a schedule-type calendar that shows the entire month on a single sheet. This way you can tell at a glance how you're doing and what your pattern is.

When should you do your aerobics, and where?

We find that exercise has the best effect on the body if it is done before dinner. The chances are that you've been hard at work all day and you're ready to just lie down and rest awhile. But if you go ahead and do your aerobics, you'll have more energy than if you had rested. Exercise perks up the body; it's a healthy stimulant. This also puts you in a proper frame of mind for dinner. Contrary to much popular opinion, aerobics doesn't cause you to eat more. As Dr. Cooper has pointed out, it tends to suppress appetites immediately afterward. Dinner is the worst meal of the day for most people, because they're used to having a huge meal. But if you exercise first, you'll have a tighter abdomen and you'll feel more like eating a *good* meal.

As far as fitness is concerned, it doesn't matter what time of day you exercise, as long as you do it regularly. But one guideline should be observed, whichever time you select: Always wait at least two hours after a meal. This is very important, for your health's sake.

Where you exercise doesn't matter, as long as you have the distance measured accurately. A good system is to check it with the automobile speedometer before you start stepping it off. For those who don't like to "just walk," we recommend driving out to the beach, if you have one, or to a lake or park or other scenic spot. Measure off a mile or two and start. Or if you're in a large city and it's inconvenient to drive elsewhere, you might find a place downtown that is safe and pleasant. Or your own neighborhood might be just right.

If you run in place, there's no problem of where, but you should purchase a special pad to protect the bones in your feet. If you run outside, it is wise to avoid running on pavement; running on concrete can inflict a condition known as "jogger's heel," affecting the Achilles tendon. Walking, though, is all right.

The main thing is to decide on a place and a time and then

do it! Don't ever postpone it for more than one day. That one day can stretch into two and three and more. Exercise should become an action that you perform automatically, just as you brush your teeth in the morning.

If you don't like to walk or jog, you might find bike riding more pleasant. Cycling may present a bit of a problem on a busy, polluted downtown street; you should look for a safe place where you can bike without stopping until you have attained your points for that day.

A few tips may prove helpful to the beginner on the aerobics program: Don't overexert yourself so that you get too tired. After you've finished your day's stint, taper off slowly; don't go into a hot room or shower immediately after exercising. Never exercise when ill or very tired. If you get behind in your program, gradually work yourself back up to where you were. Always use comfortable clothes and shoes that are suitable to the type of exercise you're doing. Take special care in hot and cold weather. If you should have a chest pain, stop. Prudence is desirable in exercise as in everything else.

There is no alternative exercise to aerobics. This doesn't mean that it need replace another exercise or sport that you enjoy. It simply means that aerobics should come first. If you go to a gym for a workout, you can jog on a treadmill first for about fifteen minutes; then go and do your gymnastics. Or if you lift weights, that's fine. Just add aerobics and continue weight-lifting. The same goes for calisthenics. Each helps to enhance the good effects of the other.

So aerobics helps prevent heart disease. Is that all? Not exactly. Exercise also helps improve the health of the teeth and gums! This is because what helps one part of the body will also help every other part.

Dr. Joseph Hrachovec, citing a University of Southern California study, reports that exercise relieves nervous tension, reduces joint stiffness, lowers fatigue and blood pressure. "It acts like a miracle drug and it's free." So if you want to take care of your teeth or your left big toe or your liver, exercise. If you're eating right and have your stress under control, you'll find that regular exercise will make everything else work better.

If you can do your aerobics outside in fresh air and sunlight, so much the better. It is helpful to get out into your environment every day. We all need sunshine. If you exercise in the sunshine without sunglasses, you are much better off. A lot is being learned about natural light. Sunglasses prevent the sun's rays from reaching the pituitary gland through the eyes. The pituitary gland apparently needs these rays to help make the body work efficiently. We know one woman in her thirties who, after throwing away her sunglasses and continuing her daily walks, began to enjoy normal menstrual periods for the first time in her life. Natural man —and woman—did not have sunglasses.

Of course, this doesn't condone the sun bakers who expose themselves to hours of direct midday summer sun. Up to an hour per day is healthy. If you're on bright snow or at a beach longer, sunglasses might be helpful.

Some of the benefits of aerobics have to do with the deep breathing that is necessary. Most of us breathe so shallowly all day that we never absorb much oxygen. No wonder clogged-up nostrils are a problem! Dr. McCamy has made a study of one hundred people who were practicing aerobics daily and eating properly, compared with one hundred others who were taking no such exercise. The number of colds in the first group plummeted almost to zero; in the other there was no change. If you're walking, running, biking, your nostrils are clear, as you breathe fully and deeply.

In another study, mental symptoms, such as depression and simple anxiety, dropped 55 percent as the result of exercise alone. Other researchers have shown a significant decrease in circulating blood fats, cholesterol and triglycerides as the result of exercise. (This drop lasted for about two days, another indication that you should exercise at least every other day.) Some diabetics on a regular exercise program have been able to reduce their insulin intake. Regular exercise also counteracts the usual aging process: Keep young with aerobics! It has been proved helpful in weight reduction. And these are only some of the known benefits.

Aerobics is needed by children and teen-agers as well as by adults. With the present-day emphasis on competitive sports in our schools, the natural order has been reversed: the fittest child receives the most attention, whereas it is the unfit who should be given more attention. We believe less emphasis should be placed on competitive sports, from which relatively few benefit physically. Instead we see no reason why schools could not have methodical personalized programs to keep all children in top physical condition. Until the schools change, the organizing of hiking clubs for children and teen-agers could partially fill this need.

After you have installed aerobics as a regular habit, you may include stretching exercises in your program. These are ideal for a warm-up routine preceding your aerobics for the day. It takes about two minutes, as you perform ten of each of the following:

1. Arm swings to the front, as far overhead and back as possible.
2. Arm swings to the back.
3. Twisters, stretching way overhead in a big circle.
4. Body swings, bending over and swinging side to side.
5. Side straddle hops.

Most of us are acquainted with these from either military, school or TV exercises. With the arm swings, you simply stretch your arms in every direction, then reverse them to swing into the opposite direction: all the way back, as far as you can, then all the way forward. Not a fast swing—it is for its stretching effect. Ten times each way.

Then do your aerobics.

Each time you do your aerobics, follow by five minutes of slower walking to cool down your system. It is not advised to stop immediately after the exercise. The cool-down walk, which is what most people think of as a gentle stroll, helps you taper off from the vigorous activity.

Then if you wish to perform more body conditioning you may add the following, building up to twenty-five of each:

1. Bent-leg sit-ups
2. Push-ups
3. Hip-ups with the arms back

These would take about five minutes for each session. But if this type of body conditioning doesn't appeal to you, you can obtain the same effect with gymnastics, tennis, golf, weight-lifting, sailing, TV exercises or horseback riding. A good hatha-yoga program is a perfect companion to aerobics. A half hour to three hours, three times weekly, should help put you in superb physical condition—if you are doing your aerobics, too.

These conditioning exercises or sports, however, are for that alone. They do *not* replace aerobics for health.

Regular stretching exercises are worth considering by everyone, young and old. They are preventive for a number of joint disorders. The most effective antidote for osteoarthritis is simply to move every joint in the body every day. It and bursitis are practically 100 percent preventable, if you merely sit on the floor once a day, every day, bending the joints a little. Every joint in your body can benefit from stretching. A good procedure is to rotate your head slowly, stretching vertebra by vertebra, then roll it forward, then back. Do the same with the hands and fingers and all other joints in the body. As with all other exercise, it is important to build up slowly.

The practice of sitting in chairs is related to the high incidence of osteoarthritis of the hip in this country. In Japan, where people sit cross-legged, it just doesn't occur. You don't have to sit on the floor to protect yourself; just bend the hips once every day in all directions, up, sideways and all the way back. Do it slowly, smoothly, stretching out. Stretching goes hand in glove with the health of your joints, and it could save the agony and staggering expense of some of the more radical treatments that have been dreamed up for osteoarthritis of the hip and other joints: cutting off the entire top of the hipbone and setting in titanium capsules and total sockets, rebuilding pelvises, and prescribing huge doses of cortisone. Osteoarthritis, and a number of other bone disorders, can be prevented by simply seeing that the body functions as it should—which costs nothing.

A cautionary note: There are a few individuals who should not participate in vigorous exercise, and if there's any doubt in your mind you should consult your physician first. If you've had a coronary within the last four weeks, if you have active congestive heart failure, if you're over 50 percent overweight, or if you have *very* high blood pressure (200/110, for instance)—these are the types of conditions that naturally would require medical attention before you would be able to exercise.

But there is almost no objection to walking, as long as you start out gently and step it up gradually. In fact, exercise is essential for many partially disabled patients. Any arthritic or any person suffering with a joint disorder *must* swim, if it is at all possible. Almost everyone can do some exercising. It improves your total health picture.

The exercise tables at the end of this chapter have been adapted from Dr. Kenneth H. Cooper's book *The New Aerobics*. To be sure you're approaching it safely, we recommend that you start in on the slowest advancing charts and work your way up slowly. If your timing automatically promotes you, that's different, but *don't push it*. Your initial timing is not important. The ultimate goal is—a change of life style.

After you have worked up to a 30-point level in your chosen activity, you may turn to the last set of tables and select a program you'd like to maintain for the rest of your life.

If you have a nonmedical excuse for not exercising, analyze it closely before you accept it as valid. Dr. Cooper, the father of aerobics, has photographs of a blind man running. One of his patients had no feet but ran anyway, using the equipment necessary.

Start by walking gently for thirty minutes tonight. Step it up briskly, then keep it up until it is a regular part of your life.

A Lifelong Exercise Program—A Complete Summary

Here is your personal outline of the total exercise program in this chapter. When you reach an optimal level, you should be able to do it all in about twenty-five or thirty minutes.

OPTIONAL

1. Warm-ups, ten of each (two minutes):
   a) Arm swings, front
   b) Arm swings, back
   c) Twisters

d) Body swings
e) Side straddle hops

IMPERATIVE

2. Your choice of aerobics. This is most important. Consult the tables in this chapter. If you are over thirty, for safety's sake you may use the over-fifty tables, which will bring you up to the optimal level gradually. It *must* be done to have the best of health. When you have worked your way up to 30 points a week, maintain that level.

3. Cool down—walking (five minutes).

OPTIONAL

4. Conditioning, twenty-five of each (five minutes):
   a) Bent-leg sit-ups
   b) Push-ups
   c) Hip-ups with arm back, or
   d) Gymnastics, tennis, golf, weights, sailing, TV exercises, horseback riding, etc. (one-half to three hours, three times weekly). These do *not* replace aerobics.

WALKING EXERCISE PROGRAM
(under 30 years of age)

STARTER

Week	Distance (miles)	Time (minutes)	Frequency (week)	Points (week)
1	1.0	15:00	5	5
2	1.0	14:00	5	10
3	1.0	13:45	5	10
4	1.5	21:30	5	15
5	1.5	21:00	5	15
6	1.5	20:30	5	15

After completing the above starter program, continue with the Category I conditioning program below.

CONDITIONING

Fitness Category I

Week	Distance (miles)	Time (minutes)	Frequency (week)	Points (week)
7	2.0	28:00	5	20
8	2.0	27:45	5	20
9	2.0	27:30	5	20
10	2.0	27:30	3	22
	and			
	2.5	33:45	2	
11	2.0	27:30	3	22
	and			
	2.5	33:30	2	
12	2.5	33:15	4	26
	and			
	3.0	41:30	1	
13	2.5	33:15	3	27
	and			
	3.0	41:15	2	
14	2.5	33:00	3	27
	and			
	3.0	40:00	2	
15	3.0	41:00	5	30
16	4.0	55:00	3	33

After completing the progressive walking program, select one of the 30-point-per-week programs.

WALKING EXERCISE PROGRAM
(age 50 and over)
STARTER

Week	Distance (miles)	Time (minutes)	Frequency (week)	Points (week)
1	1.0	18:30	5	5
2	1.0	16:30	5	5
3	1.0	15:00	5	5
4	1.5	24:30	5	7½
5	1.5	23:00	5	7½
6	1.5	22:30	5	7½

After completing the above starter program, continue with the Category I conditioning program below.

CONDITIONING

Fitness Category I

Week	Distance (miles)	Time (minutes)	Frequency (week)	Points (week)
7	2.0	32:00	5	10
8	2.0	31:00	5	10
9	2.5	38:30	5	12½
10	2.0 and	28:45	2	15½
	2.5	27:30	3	
11	2.0 and	28:30	3	17
	2.5	37:00	2	
12	2.5 and	36:00	3	21
	3.0	44:30	2	
13	2.0 and	28:00	2	26
	3.0	43:15	3	
14	2.5 and	35:00	3	27
	3.0	43:00	2	
15	3.0	43:00	5	30
16	4.0	57:00	3	33

After completing the progressive walking program, select one of the 30-point-per-week programs.

RUNNING EXERCISE PROGRAM
(age 50 and over)

STARTER *

Week	Distance (miles)	Time (minutes)	Frequency (week)	Points (week)
1	1.0	18:30	5	5
2	1.0	17:00	5	5
3	1.0	16:00	5	5
4	1.0	15:00	5	5
5	1.0	14:15	5	10
6	1.0	13:45	5	10

* Start the program by walking, then walk and run, or run, as is necessary to meet the changing time goals.

After completing the above starter program, continue with the Category I conditioning program below.

CONDITIONING

Fitness Category I

Week	Distance (miles)	Time (minutes)	Frequency (week)	Points (week)
7	1.5	22:00	5	15
8	1.5	20:30	5	15
9	1.5	19:30	5	15
10	1.0	11:30	1	15
	and			
	1.5	18:30	4	
11	1.0	10:45	1	21
	and			
	1.5	17:30	4	
12	1.0	10:15	1	21
	and			
	1.5	16:30	4	
13	1.5	16:00	3	27½
	and			
	2.0	22:00	2	
14	1.0	9:45	2	29
	and			
	2.0	21:15	3	
15	1.5	15:05	2	30
	and			
	2.0	20:30	3	
16	1.0	9:30	1	34
	and			
	1.5	14:25	2	
	and			
	2.0	19:55	2	

After completing the progressive running program, select one of the 30-point-per-week programs.

CYCLING EXERCISE PROGRAM
(age 50 and over)

S T A R T E R

Week	Distance (miles)	Time (minutes)	Frequency (week)	Points (week)
1	2.0	11:30	5	5
2	2.0	10:30	5	5
3	2.0	10:00	5	5
4	3.0	16:00	5	7½
5	3.0	15:30	5	7½
6	3.0	15:00	5	7½

After completing the above starter program, continue with the Category I conditioning program below.

C O N D I T I O N I N G

Fitness Category I

Week	Distance (miles)	Time (minutes)	Frequency (week)	Points (week)
7	4.0	21.00	5	10
8	4.0	20.00	5	10
9	5.0	26:30	5	12½
10	5.0 and	25:00	1	14½
	6.0	32:00	4	
11	5.0 and	25:00	3	18½
	7.0	39:30	2	
12	7.0	38:00	4	22
13	5.0 and	24:00	2	24½
	8.0	42:00	3	
14	8.0 and	40:00	3	28
	10.0	57:30	1	
15	10.0	55:00	4	34
16	12.0	65:00	3	31½

After completing the progressive cycling program, select one of the 30-point-per-week programs.

SWIMMING EXERCISE PROGRAM—Overhand Crawl*
(age 50 and over)

STARTER

Week	Distance (yards)	Time (minutes)	Frequency (week)	Points (week)
1	100	2:30	5	4
2	150	3:45	5	5
3	175	4:15	5	6
4	200	4:45	5	7½
5	200	4:30	5	7½
6	200	4:15	5	7½

* Breaststroke is less demanding and so is backstroke. Butterfly is considerably more demanding.

After completing the above starter program, continue with the Category I conditioning program below.

CONDITIONING

Fitness Category I

Week	Distance (yards)	Time (minutes)	Frequency (week)	Points (week)
7	200	5:45	5	10
8	250	5:30	5	10
9	300	7:15	5	12½
10	300	6:45	5	12½
11	400	9:45	5	17½
12	400 and	9:30	2	19
	500	12:00	3	
13	400 and	9:15	2	22
	600	13:45	3	
14	500 and	11:30	2	26
	700	16:30	3	
15	700	16:00	5	30
16	800	18:00	4	30

After completing the progressive swimming program, select one of the 30-point-per-week programs.

STATIONARY RUNNING EXERCISE PROGRAM
(age 50 and over)

STARTER

Week	Duration (minutes)	Steps (minutes*)	Frequency (week)	Points (week)
1	1:30	70–80	5	—
2	2:30	70–80	5	4
3	2:30	70–80	5	5
4	5:00	70–80	5	7½
5	5:00	70–80	5	7½
6	5:00	70–80	5	7½

* Count only when the left foot hits the floor. Feet must be brought at least eight inches from the floor.

After completing the above starter program, continue with the Category I conditioning program below.

CONDITIONING

Fitness Category I

Week	Duration (minutes)	Steps (minutes*)	Frequency (week)	Points (week)
7	7:30	70–80	5	11¼
8	7:30	70–80	5	11¼
9	10:00	70–80	5	15
10	10:00	70–80	5	15
11	10:00	70–80	5	15
12	12:30	70–80	5	18¾
13	10:00 (A.M.) and	70–80	2	23¼
	10:00 (P.M.) and	70–80		
	12:30	70–80	3	
14	10:00 (A.M.) and	70–80	2	25½
	10:00 (P.M.) and	70–80		
	15:00	70–80	3	

* Count only when the left foot hits the floor. Feet must be brought at least eight inches from the floor.

Week	Duration (minutes)	Steps (minutes*)	Frequency (week)	Points (week)
15	12:30 (A.M.) and	70–80	2	28½
	12:30 (P.M.) and			
	15:00	70–80	3	
16	20:00	70–80	4	32

* Count only when the left foot hits the floor. Feet must be brought at least eight inches from the floor.

After completing the progressive stationary running program, select one of the 30-point-per-week programs.

SUGGESTED PROGRESSIVE WALKING PROGRAM
FOR CARDIAC PATIENTS

Moderate Disease

Weeks	Distance (miles)	Time Goal (minutes)	Frequency (week)	Points (week)
1–2	1.0	24:00	5	—
3–4	1.0	20:00	5	—
5–6	1.0	18:00	5	5
7–8	1.0	16:00	5	5
9–10	1.5	25:00	5	7½
11–12	1.5	24:00	5	7½
13–14	2.0	33:00	5	10
15–16	2.0	32:00	5	10
17–18	1.5 and	23:00	2	10½
	2.5	40:00	3	
19–20	1.5 and	22:30	2	12
	3.0	47:00	3	
21–22	2.5 and	38:00	2	15½
	3.5	54:00	3	
23–24	2.5 and	36:00	3	21
	3.0	44:00	2	
25–26	3.0 and	43:15	3	26
	4.0	61:00	2	
27–28	3.0 and	43:15	3	26
	4.0	60:00	2	
29–30	3.0	43:00	5	30
31–32	4.0	57:45	3	33

Thereafter maintain one of the last two schedules as a permanent form of exercise.

Once you have worked up to 30 points a week, you may use any combination of these.

Walking only is recommended for post-cardiac patients or those over sixty.

MAINTENANCE PROGRAMS

Fitness level is satisfactory at the outset. The only requirement is to maintain fitness, using one of the following exercise programs.

	Distance (miles)	Time Requirement (minutes)	Frequency (week)	Points (week)
Walking	2.0	24:00–26:00	8	32
	or 3.0	36:00–43:30	5	30
	or 4.0	58:00–79:59	5	35
	or 4.0	48:00–58:00	3	33
Running	1.0	6:30– 7:59	6	30
	or 1.5	12:00–14:59	5	30
	or 1.5	9:45–11:59	4	30
	or 2.0	16:00–19:59	4	36
	or 2.0	13:00–15:59	3	33
Cycling	5.0	15:00–19:59	6	30
	or 6.0	18:00–23:59	5	30
	or 7.0	21:00–27:59	4	36
	or 8.0	24:00–31:59	3	31

	Distance (yards)			
Swimming	500	8:20–12:59	8	32
	or 600	10:00–14:59	6	30
	or 800	13:20–19:59	4	30
	or 1000	16:40–24:59	3	31½

	Duration (minutes)	Steps (minutes*)	Frequency (week)	Points (week)
Stationary Running	10:00 in A.M. and	70–80	5	30
	10:00 in P.M.	70–80		
	or 15:00	70–80	7	30
	or 15:00	80–90	5	30
	or 20:00	70–80	4	32

* Count only when the left foot hits the floor. Feet must be brought at least eight inches from the floor.

Handball	40:00	—	5	30
Basketball	50:00	—	4	30
Squash	70:00	—	3	30

6

How to Relax and Reduce Stress

If you're on full nutrition and exercising regularly, you've already done a lot to reduce stress in your life. A person in top physiological condition can handle the stresses of life more effectively.

If you add the stress-reducing techniques in this chapter, you should spiral up to optimal. In his clinic, Dr. McCamy has found that patients practicing the entire Human Life Styling program can reduce their nervous symptoms by 90 percent.

Two tools for changing your stress response will be presented:

1. Mental sets that will enable you to approach the stresses of life in a more realistic manner.

2. Relaxation techniques to help your body and mind relax and recover from the ravages of stress.

In addition, we recommend a minimum of two weeks vacation every year, as well as one day of vacation every month. Each should be taken in a situation that would be conducive to natural rhythm completely breaking with your workaday routine.

Emotional stress can cause the body to deteriorate through

a complex, interrelated mechanism. Stress as the result of circulating thoughts may begin in the cerebrum, which is the thinking part of the brain. The cerebrum, though, may affect the hypothalamus, which directly controls the endocrine glands, the automatic nervous system and the chemical balance of the body. You can literally think yourself sick.

Prolonged mental strain can lead to physical breakdown, which in turn contributes to another decline in mental health. It becomes a vicious spiral down. Emotional stress is just as real to our bodies as any kind of physical stress. Overly stressed people are more susceptible to coronaries, early strokes and cancer. When you're under stress, you're more likely to contract a sore throat or a cold than at other times; your need for vitamin C, as well as other vitamins, may be several times that which you'd normally require.

When you feel the effects of emotional stress, your body is out of balance. Cells are actually deteriorating. The dangers are not imaginary. Stress is invariably a factor in any emotional disease we have studied, but once it starts to spiral down, physiological reactions may join in to worsen the bad situation.

Until recently the physiological bases of emotions and stress have taken a back seat to the psychological theories of mental disease. Yet with the intimate, interlocking status of body and mind, one cannot be separated from, or ranked above, the other. What happens to the cells in the brain will have a profound effect on the behavior of the individual.

In other words, the body and the mind are the same. The body affects the mind. The mind affects the body.

Whether the trouble originates in the mind or derives from nonmental sources, it can come to have a life of its own as it rapidly involves both body and mind. For instance, when a patient complains of abdominal cramps, the doctor may find nothing organically wrong. Often even the patient will believe it's psychosomatic. "It's only my imagination that I have pains." Although such pains may sometimes derive from a worried imagination, the pains are real and the bowel is actually deteriorating. If it was precipitated primarily by emotional stress, how the patient handles that stress will determine whether this early symptom leads to a major organic breakdown or if he recovers and guides his body back into balance.

Although psychological counseling may help you if you are under emotional stress, the emphasis in this chapter will be on what you can do for yourself.

Emotional stress is subjective. It is *how* we respond to a given event. Circulating thoughts may bring on the stress. The more we control our minds, so as to curtail these circulating thoughts, the less we are bothered by emotional stress. This is one reason two people may react quite differently to the same potentially stressful situation.

As an example, let's assume there are four hundred people in a movie theater. Suddenly it becomes known that fire has broken out. The alarm spreads quickly so that everyone knows. Possibly 10 percent of the audience would panic and run out screaming. Or try to run out. But another 10 percent or so would probably walk out calmly, if they weren't swamped by the stampeders, and announce, "The theater is on fire. Call the fire department. Look for the fire extinguishers. Get some water." The other 80 percent would be somewhere in between the two extremes.

Same event, same stress. What mattered was how the individual responded to it. There was a choice—as there is in almost every experience that occurs in our lives. Even in the most serious crises of life we have a choice of behavior. If one's mate suffered a coronary or a stroke, one person might run screaming into the street without communicating with anyone or might crumple into fear, too paralyzed to act. Another, calmer person would handle it in a totally opposite manner, thinking, "Well, it looks like a stroke. What can I do about it? First I'll call the doctor." That person would respond reasonably to the emergency, do what could be done and maintain control over his or her actions. Obviously, the latter response is the one to be expected from a truly normal person.

To better control the stress in your life, it will help to discipline yourself to review this program daily. It is a part of your new approach to health. The initial time it takes will decrease as the new life style becomes an intimate part of you. Eventually it will become second nature and will require no conscious effort or time on your part.

At first it will take lots of practice, but just as you needn't change overnight in the other aspects of the program, you also have the opportunity to reduce gradually your response to stresses.

The goal of this chapter is to supply you with the techniques that will enable you to grow toward becoming a truly normal person. When stress appears in the life of a normal person he responds to it appropriately. He does what he can do. He acts rather than worries. When that's done, he's no longer under stress.

Mental Sets for Reducing Stress

Every person has to a large degree the ability to control his or her actions consciously. You can set your mind on a particular approach to life. In fact, every day we make conscious and unconscious choices. By becoming aware of our choices, we can work to ensure that they serve to relax us and reduce our stresses, rather than work against us, as our choices so often do.

The twelve mental sets that follow can be used as guide-

lines to improve your emotional life style. Read each one
slowly. Digest it, then go on to the next one. Read them over
each day, if need be, and think of how they can fit into your
daily life. Then practice them and gradually weave them into
your life fabric. They will become part of you. They will
be you.

1. There is no outside emotional stress; there is only my
   subjective response to a situation, which I can learn to
   control.
2. I will do one thing at a time.
3. I will do the best I can about a situation, and then I
   won't worry about it.
4. I will express my feelings honestly to other people.
5. I will think and live positively, committing myself to the
   highest I can be; even from "bad" experiences I can
   learn lessons of growth.
6. I will treat *all* others, including children, with the respect I wish for myself.
7. If I or my mate should be dissatisfied with our sexual
   relationship, I will take steps to improve it.
8. Death is a normal, inevitable part of human life; I will
   face this fact and accept the world as it is.
9. I will be aware of my own needs, rather than those inspired by competition.
10. I will not feel closed in, but will realize that there are
    always options.
11. By keeping in touch with my body and its needs, I will
    choose to be well and happy.
12. I will live in the golden now.

With these twelve mental sets we can, to a large degree,
create our own world, emotionally speaking. As Ken Keyes,
Jr., has said, "A loving person lives in a loving world, a

hostile person lives in a hostile world: Everyone you meet is your mirror."

This is not to say that you should ever expect perfection of yourself, even after years of working zealously to improve yourself. It is well to tell yourself each day: *I won't chastise myself if I act otherwise—this is "where I am" at the moment in my growth.* It is important to allow yourself and others the freedom to be imperfect.

Some of the mental sets will be needed more often than others. Especially that of doing one thing at a time. You can use it throughout every day and eliminate a major source of stress. Isolate one item on your agenda, do it well, and go on to the next item. Give your undivided concentration to what you are doing at the time. If you have two or more problems, decide which is more important and work on it before turning to another. If you read, just read. If you're having a conversation, talk when it's your turn and when the other is talking, listen completely. When you're driving, just drive and be alert: no talking, no radio listening, no circulating thoughts. This alone will relieve tension. If a thought comes, let it glide on through. You'll be a calmer and safer driver. Do this in your leisure hours and in your job. You'll be surprised at how it helps to simplify life. Because it helps you to set priorities, you'll accomplish more. You can do only so many things in a day. Do what is important. Save the rest for another day, if at all. A lot of irrelevance will fade from your life.

As for a complex task or problem, you might simplify it by doing one step at a time. This breaks it down so that you won't have to concentrate on all its ramifications at once.

Worry is abnormal. There is only so much you can do about a given situation or problem. Do what you sensibly can, then turn to something else. Worry can be programmed out by repeating with each problem, "I have a problem here. What can I do about it? I intend to do the best I can. That's all I can do." The person who does that will be better off when the chips are down, in a true crisis.

Most of us are taught from early childhood "not to hurt people's feelings." When you don't tell someone how you really feel, you're depriving him or her of the benefit of honesty. For you, suppressed feelings may cause enough internal stress to leave you functioning below your optimum; over a long period of time, it could be a factor in serious disease. One definition of an ulcer is that it is a repressed feeling. If you don't want to do something or if you don't like something, say so. It's possible to be both honest and gracious.

Every day offers unique opportunities, which a positive outlook helps us to see. Even setbacks and disappointments can become opportunities, as learning experiences. Gain something valuable out of every one. It's always there.

The only way to be respected by others as a loving person is to be that loving person in your transactions with them. This is especially true of children. Particularly our own children. The way we treat them will determine to a large extent what kind of people they will become as adults. A child from the toddler years on deserves to be treated with the dignity and respect due a full human being, which he or she is.

A good technique for attaining objectivity in dealing with one's own children is to think: How would I treat them if they weren't even related to me, if they were the governor's children—or if they were adult bankers in the community? The same technique could be applied to dealing with one's mate or parents.

Sex is central to our lives, yet unsatisfactory sexual relationships persist. Because they are personal, sexual problems are often suffered secretly. Men and women in their seventies have never been asked a question about their sex lives by professionals, because even doctors are uncomfortable in such a role.

An unsatisfactory sexual life can be a source of deep stress. If either of the partners is dissatisfied in any way, he or she should bring it up with the other. Sex is one of the more difficult topics to discuss honestly, but it's worth it. Cooperate to enjoy what you have, and can have. If necessary, compromise on frequency of sexual relations. After all, the gentleness, the touching and the intimacy are the important things.

If you have problems that you can't resolve yourselves, seek professional counseling. A physician or a psychologist may be helpful.

Fear of death brings stress to many people. It may be quite deep, repressed to the point where it's never talked about. We have no control over death, except to the extent of delaying it temporarily by maintaining healthy bodies.

Death comes along like everything else in the world. It's not bad. It's not good. It just is. Accepting calmly the fact that you, too, will die someday can help make you far more effective in life. The person who learns to accept the inevitable can divert his energies toward changing the things that he can change.

As Dr. Martin Luther King, Jr., said, "No man is free until he is free of the fear of death."

We live in a highly competitive society in which one is constantly tempted to compare oneself with others. But anytime you compare yourself to someone else, you're putting yourself down. There's no way the competitive person can win. He's always vying with somebody. He never feels quite adequate. He is letting his life be shaped by the accomplishments or status of others. He has lost control of directing his own life. A normal person wants what he needs, instead of needing what he wants.

"To be uptight over what you don't have," said Ken Keyes, Jr., "is to waste what you do have."

If you feel tense or nerve-shredded in your job, something is wrong somewhere. Check out the trouble. The chances are that you can do something about it. If it can't be resolved through honest discussion with the appropriate people, maybe it's in the job itself. Maybe you're not working at what you enjoy most. If so, then try to do what you would like to do.

Remember the "Peter principle" regarding why things go wrong. One reason is that people are promoted to the level of their incompetence. The McCamy corollary to the Peter principle is: Drop to the level of your competence. If you were a happy mechanic until your promotion, then be a mechanic again instead of a foreman. The loss in salary might be made up in a gain in life, as well as by quality of life. If your hours are too long, drop down to the number of hours you are comfortable working. If you can't do that, consider changing your job. Our options are more numerous than we usually realize. Suicides are caused by failure to see the options.

Be a friend to your body. Give it work, food and rest. Don't let yourself become excessively fatigued from either work or play. Proper sleep is a resistance factor. You must have enough, to allow your body time to recuperate from the day's exertions. Each person requires from seven to nine hours of sleep; a few, perhaps, may find six to be enough. Find the sleep pattern that fits you and adhere to it; usually that's the amount of time you sleep when there's no alarm clock to awaken you.

Be aware of your body. When an urge to move your bowels occurs, go to the bathroom that moment. Ignoring such urges over a period of time may lead to irregularity and constipation. A normal person has regular bowel movements.

By befriending your body and by maintaining a healthy mental outlook, you can also probably prevent major accidents. Dr. McCamy has observed, in his own patients, that almost every accident was "wished" by the victim, either consciously or subconsciously. Approximately half of our automobile accidents, for example, are alcohol-related; the other half are frequently referable to depressed or accident-prone drivers. Of the alcohol-related incidents, two-thirds are linked to problem drinkers, one-third to young excessive drinkers acting out unresolved problems, as well as physical possibilities such as hypoglycemia and inadequate exercise (which could lead to a lack of alertness and poor coordination). Nearly all these accidents, we believe, could be prevented. We can choose to be safe, and generally speaking we can also choose to be well and happy.

Time itself becomes a source of stress to many people when they distort reality by living in either the past or the future. But time is always *now*. The past has vanished. The future is an unborn tomorrow. Focus on the present and live in the golden now. It is the only real time we have. We cannot be happy yesterday. We cannot be happy tomorrow. But we can be happy today. Relish each golden moment as a gift of the ever-flowing now.

In shop, office and kitchen, this can be translated as being work-oriented rather than goal-oriented. Work for the pleasure of the work itself, doing what is appropriate. Goals can be planned in ten minutes each day or in one hour every week. That leaves the mind free, the rest of the time, to do the daily work. Monthly and annual master goal sessions may be helpful. Decide on goals, then do the necessary work, excluding all extraneous circulating thoughts.

Most work is of an automatic nature. The less we think about it, the more we get done. Even repetitive types of work can be rewarding, rather than boring, if one relaxes and blanks out everything but the work at hand. A worker in a factory assembly line could become a very advanced person emotionally simply by getting in touch with himself, blanking out all irrelevancies and doing his work well. At the end of the day he would be relaxed and stress-free as he continued his life in the wondrous present.

You can do it yourself, no matter what you do for a living.

Remember to *be here now.*

The Real You

The twelve mental sets may not only help you attain a richer emotional life style, they may also help you put experiences in their proper perspective.

The real you is so strong that you can handle anything life brings you. Your security is in becoming aware of that ability, which is the basic power of your life.

Others have found this to be so, in moments of despair, merely by changing their mental sets. Byron W., a stockbroker, faced what he considered a catastrophe when the market dropped alarmingly. Suddenly he was out of a job. "My wife is ready to leave me. I've lost my job. I'm going to kill myself," he wailed plaintively.

"What's the wildest thing you'd like to do?" he was asked.

He stopped short and gave it serious thought.

"I'd like to run a restaurant," he said.

"Where's the wildest place you'd like to live?"

"I've always wanted to live in Rio."

"Well, new restaurants open every day. It takes money, but meanwhile you wouldn't starve in this country."

But Byron refused to be distracted by this new thought for long. He returned to his earlier theme.

"There's nothing I can do. I'm living in a $150,000 house, the market is busted, I have no income. I'm ruined."

"Well, what's wrong with living in a $20,000 house? And, you realize, you could sell your house and live for a year in Rio while you're rearranging your life."

Again he stopped. He had never thought of that. Nor had he ever considered the possibility of moving elsewhere, to another state or even another city.

He sold his house, moved to another community and bought a $20,000 house. With money left over from his house sale he bought a sailboat and enjoyed the sun and the sea. His wife had never worked before, but she had always wanted to. For a while Byron took care of the children and kept the house, and she worked as a restaurant hostess and loved it.

Another potential suicide, Dr. V., had his license to practice medicine revoked because of drug abuse. He had built up a God image of himself over the years from overidentifying with his work. When he lost his practice he was shattered. It was as if he had fallen from God to nothing.

His perspective was awry and he was on the verge of destroying himself. The very thought of doing something less than his exalted role dictated had never occurred to him. Most tragic mental sets are inflexible.

It was suggested that he could live anywhere. He still had money. He had a great deal of training behind him. He was married, but the children were grown and no longer at home. He had a long line of options open to him. He could teach biology, work in a hospital, study, travel for a year, do social work, work in an underdeveloped country that was short on doctors, or work for an insurance company that wouldn't require a license. He finally took a position as a paramedical administrator in a hospital. But until someone had pointed out the choices life offered him, his had been shotgun vision.

Others have headed off crises by changing their mental sets and life styles. An engineer who had been in the aerospace industry for nearly a decade had been under great stress for years. When a cutback came, his stress was heightened. Most of all he feared a layoff. He was so wrapped up in his job that he didn't know anything else.

His wife had anxiously watched his tensions mount over the years. One day she suggested, "Let's move to another town and get away from it!" He gave it serious consideration and they did just that. He liked working with his hands and dealing with people. He got a job driving a cab and started doing carpentry work in his shop at home, and became happier than he had ever been as an engineer.

Once liberated from their abnormal mental sets, these individuals had found in their real selves a resilience that made their lives more meaningful.

Alpha, Beta and You

Almost every abnormal mental set and every source of emotional stress comes from the thought process. If you'll quit thinking, you won't have any stresses. This requires a total blanking out of the mind. Then there is no thought and, therefore, no emotional stress. Stress becomes an abstraction. You're just being what you are.

Blanking out the mind is a concept foreign to most of us. We feel we ought to be talking, reading, working, actively doing something when we're relaxing. It is a way of life in the West and especially in the United States, where, as historian Walter Prescott Webb has remarked, our religion is work. It is a phenomenon of the frontier. We even tend to look upon meditation as a thought process. We're supposed to be "doing something" or "thinking" all the time. This is why it is that many people who consider themselves meditating are really *thinking* meditation. Even then their minds are taken over by the thought process.

The need for the type of relaxation technique to be described in this chapter is based upon scientific study of the brain as well as observation of meditation steps from some of the world's religions. Whether it has a religious orientation or not depends on you. At the basic level, it doesn't relate to religious concepts. It can be equally beneficial to anyone in either an Eastern or a Western religion, or to someone with no religion. You can look upon it as merely a mental exercise or as a step toward oneness with the universe.

The electrical cycles of the brain can be measured in their several speeds and intensities. Our wide-awake brain waves are called beta and they race along at from 14 to 32 cycles per second. People who are under constant stress, whose worries inspire constantly circulating thoughts, never tune out of the active beta state during their waking hours.

This is abnormal. The intellect is a computer that is supposed to be turned on when we need it to solve a problem. Yet many of us have our beta computer working all the time, worrying about what happened yesterday and what will happen tomorrow.

Alpha is a lower range of brain activity, with 7 to 14 cycles per second, a very slow, even rate in which you're not thinking but you're awake. Many students of the human mind believe that alpha is the natural state of man or of any animal. Their theory is that only in the last several thousand years has the conscious mind, or beta, taken over. As you become more and more relaxed, as logical thoughts begin to disappear, such as in the twilight zone preceding sleep, alpha waves appear in the brain. Recent research indicates that a person can reduce stress and become more effective by guiding his brain waves into alpha. It may be opening the door to our deepest level of creativity.

On a slower level, the mind loses consciousness in theta,

with 4 to 7 cycles per second, and goes into a deep sleep in delta, ranging from ½ to 4 cycles per second.

There are a number of reasons why it is desirable to go into alpha state every day. It blanks out stress, which is usually reward enough for "just doing nothing" several minutes daily. It also has some measurable physical benefits. Both high and low blood pressures have been returned to normal through alpha state relaxation. Perhaps the explanation lies in the fact that with minimal stress, the body is free to work at its ideal functional level. After habitual daily sessions in alpha state, blood pressure becomes permanently normal. Exactly how it works we don't know. It may be because of that thirty minutes a day in alpha or it may be due to a decrease in the person's general life stress. Whatever is the reason, another bonus has been experienced, for patients with lowered stress response had lower blood cholesterol. It may be that alpha sessions can indirectly help regulate cholesterol levels.

In one study in which the participants performed relaxation techniques consisting of repeating the words of a monitor, significant improvement in drug use was achieved. At the beginning of the study, 86 percent of the subjects were taking drugs such as heroin or alcohol, "acid" or "speed" or barbiturates, or were smoking marijuana. After they had spent fifteen minutes a day with the monitor for one month, the use of drugs had diminished to less than 50 percent. After six months, drug use was less than 20 percent.

Using the relaxation technique we will describe shortly, Dr. McCamy has found in his clinic that the number of nervous symptoms in a patient declines progressively. Month by month, the patient grows more in touch with himself and the world around him. He has the same job as before, the same family, but now he doesn't sweat things as much as he did. He begins to see life in a more natural light. He alters his pattern of excessive thinking and stops racing his brain in a cacophony of beta waves all day.

Thinking is what wears us out. You may never have heard that before.

A Relaxation Technique Anyone Can Do

In Aleksandr I. Solzhenitsyn's novel *The Cancer Ward,* there is a scene in which an old doctor relaxes, motionless, in a rocking chair for a long time, nourishing "unmuddied, unfrozen and undistorted the image of eternity that sits within each person." It is like "a silver moon in a calm pond." He seems to have been in the alpha state.

You need at least thirty minutes every day in the alpha state, awake but not thinking. When you use the relaxation technique, all the mental sets will make more sens^. Do this every day and you'll be moving toward a stress-free state in which you are aware of your ability to control yourself and your own mind. Anyone who can count to ten can do it.

If you have someone who will read the next few pages to you, it might prove easier to absorb the routine at first. If you're working on it by yourself, you can read it and then go back to practice the steps.

First, make yourself comfortable. Sit in a chair, with your feet on the floor; if you sit on the floor, cross-legged, place your back against the wall. Keep your back straight.

Try not to move during the exercise. If your ear itches, ignore it. If you finally can't stand it, go ahead and scratch it, but first try not to.

Place your hands in your lap, with your thumbs together. This will provide a slight bit of tension at that spot and you won't go to sleep. Focus your eyes on your left hand and maintain them there. Without any conscious thought, hold your gaze on your left hand throughout this exercise.

Now take a huge, deep, full, slow breath. As you inhale, count One to yourself. All the way in. Then, slowly, exhale, all the way out, and count Two to yourself. Silently. Another inhale is Three, out is Four. Quiet, deep breaths. In, Five. Out, Six. In, Seven. Out, Eight. In is Nine, out is Ten.

Keep counting. When you get to Ten, start over at One. Slow, gentle breaths now.

If you lose count, start over at One. Just count your breaths. If a thought comes, don't acknowledge it but don't fight it either. Let it pass on through as if it were a gentle breeze wafting through your hair. Just go on counting your breaths. Let any thoughts float through your head and go on out. Don't take hold of them. Don't acknowledge sounds; let them float on through, too. Simply go on counting your breaths.

Any odors or sounds or feelings or thoughts don't matter. Don't acknowledge them. Don't fight them either. Keep your eyes focused on your left hand. Just count your breaths.

When you get to Ten, start over at One. If you lose count, start over at One.

[If a monitor is reading this, let a large gap of silence intervene here, as the exercise continues.]

Just count your breaths. Be aware of nothing but your breath. There is nothing else you have to do. Just relax, as you are. There is no stress because there is no thought. Things are just the way they are. Keep counting your breaths while I talk. Don't listen to me. Just count your breaths. Don't acknowledge any sounds or smells or voices.

This technique, done every day, gives you freedom from stress and gives you an awareness of who you are. You'll get in touch with your normal inner self. You'll function as a normal human being if this exercise is done every day. After a while you'll want to do this exercise every day. The relaxa-

tion and the pleasure coming from it more than justify the small amount of time required. You'll feel better, look better, be more relaxed, and your life will be fuller. Every day for thirty minutes you'll just count your breaths, giving your-self this gift of time.

Just keep counting your breaths. There is no stress, nothing you have to do. Just . . . be . . . here . . . now. Let thoughts go through. Return to counting your breaths. When you get to Ten, start over at One. If you lose count, start back at One.

This counting of your breaths, with daily aerobic exercise and a natural diet, will give you a full, completely healthy life.

Start taking deeper breaths now, deep full breaths. Keep counting. Long exhales and deep breaths. Feel your lungs expand. Blow all the air out. Feel the relaxation go all over you.

Now, when you want to, after some deep breaths, you can stop counting and look up. The practice exercise is over. How do you feel?

This breath-counting exercise can be done with the eyes open or closed. We prefer the eyes-open method. Although at first it may seem easier to practice with eyes closed, we find that this may encourage too many thoughts for some people, as they perceive a mental screen. But if you open your eyes and focus on one point, your awareness remains there and is easier to control. As you focus on your left hand and count your breaths, you're doing quite a lot. Doing both these things mechanically helps to crowd out any itinerant thoughts.

This relaxation exercise will take you into alpha. After about three months of thirty-minute daily exercises, you can start counting only your exhales, further simplifying the pro-cedure. The step after that is to just be aware of your breaths, without counting. Or you don't have to go any further than the initial lesson; just keep counting your breaths from now on and you'll have a perfectly good stress-reduction program.

There are scores of other meditation or alpha-reaching techniques. You can count backward. There is the Silva Mind Control program. You can focus on color, or flashing lights. You can accomplish the same thing by watching the sun set and in silent prayer. But as long as the intellect is working, you're back in beta. If you are thinking, "This is a beautiful sunset," you are not in alpha. If you are verbalizing while in prayer, you're not praying, you're thinking; you're sending but not receiving. If you should use prayer as your alpha state session, you might try praying with your eyes open to see if you can.

If you are now using a technique other than the one described here, by all means keep using it. Counting your breaths just happens to be a system that works. It gives you something to hang on to in the early stages. Most meditation techniques start with breath-counting, because it's such a reliable training approach.

You can use the breath-counting technique at other parts of the day as well. If you have insomnia, count your breaths up to ten and then start over again. You'll soon fall asleep, for this will blank out all competing thoughts that might keep you awake, while the rhythm of the counting and the awareness of your breathing will lull you to sleep.

You can also use it during the day. At work, if it seems that you suddenly have so many problems you don't know what to do next, just go blank for a few minutes, counting your breaths, getting rid of your worries momentarily. Do the same if you experience frustration or are violently angry. The mind welcomes a respite. The solution usually follows. As you learn to go into the alpha state readily, you'll probably notice a significant tranquillity in your life. Alpha is always there, within easy reach, whenever you need it, and like exercise, it's free.

When is the best time to practice the technique? It doesn't matter. A convenient time is after aerobics, to combine both. After exercising you're breathing deeply and it feels good to sit down and rest anyway. One can blend naturally into the other. Other people enjoy it in the morning; it helps them prepare for the day's work. Still others use it in the evening and flow smoothly on to sleep afterward. This is fine as long as you remain in the alpha state for as much of your thirty-minute daily quota as you can. We need sleep, which is theta, but we need alpha, too, for full health.

In the West we have developed a habit of learning *about* things and not doing them. This is the source of a lot of our stresses. The main thing about this thirty-minute relaxation technique is to use it, or a reasonable substitute, every day!

Your Check List for Stress Reduction

Following this guide daily will help you to reduce your response to stress and restore your body's natural rhythm. The point system for this portion of Human Life Styling is optional. A total of 30 points, on a daily basis, is both desirable and perfect. You should make an effort to attain this every day of the week.

Points

- Thirty continuous minutes daily; a relaxation technique of 20
  counting breaths, going blank, watching the sunset or silent
  prayer ($\frac{2}{3}$ point per minute).
- Do one thing at a time, and review the twelve mental sets 10
  daily.

SUPPLEMENTAL

- A minimum of two weeks' vacation per year, plus one day
  per month, in a situation conducive to the natural rhythm.

7

Does It Work? / Case Histories

In this chapter we will present patients' stories as evidence that Human Life Styling works. These cases, though, may not convince you that you will be able to practice all four facets of the program where you live. If you lived on a farm in a Colorado mountain valley and could grow your food, breathe plenty of fresh, crisp air while exercising, and keep yourself free of stress, there would be no problem. But what if you live in a large city?

Let's say you live in an apartment in New York City. (Maybe you do.) If you can follow the Human Life Styling program in such an environment, you should be able to adhere to it anywhere. How would you lead a natural life there?

We will break down the four parts of the program.

Nutrition—First you can eliminate the susceptibility factors, such as sugar, smoking, drugs, all refined carbohydrates and snack foods. You can live anywhere and do this much, which is quite a lot. Then you start looking for resistance factors. You can buy eggs, cheese, milk and fresh vegetables at food stores. Most large cities have fresh fruit and vegetable markets. You can probably find fresh fish, fowl and meats.

As next-best choice, you can use fresh-frozen foods. You can even sprout some seeds at home. You can find whole grains and bread, as well as unhydrogenated oils and peanut butter, in health food stores. You can always buy supplements. Once you start looking for what your body needs, you'll start finding it; after a while, it'll be easier.

Exercise—There's Central Park in the daytime. Most cities have several parks that are safe. You can almost always walk in any city, if you choose your time and place. Central Park has bicycle paths. Instead of fighting the lunch-hour rush, you can drink juice and run or walk. There are also spas, Y's or health clubs where you can swim, cycle or do treadmill exercises. As a last resort, you can *always* purchase a sponge rubber pad and run in place at your apartment.

Stress Reduction—You can practice your mental sets anywhere, anytime. To prevent your becoming alienated from your fellow man, take the excitement of the city in stride. Do the relaxation technique every day at home. All the equipment you need for this is already in your brain.

Ecology—There's plenty to do for the environment in New York, as in any other city of the world. It shouldn't be difficult to find some kindred souls.

You now have the tools with which to change your prospects for illness. The more you do to change your health habits, the healthier your life style will be.

On the basis of Dr. McCamy's records, it seems clear that a person's health improvement is directly related to how faithfully he or she follows all four paths in Human Life Styling. When a patient first joins the program, a standard questionnaire is administered on which he lists all his symptoms. From nine to eighteen months later, as part of a repeat work-up, the questionnaire is readministered. The table below depicts an estimate of how approximately one thousand patients have responded. As can be seen, about 25 percent of the patients rated "Good" performances. That is to say, they did practically all the items on the check lists. These are the "stars" of Human Life Styling, and they averaged 90 percent reduction in symptoms.

Half of the patients, or 50 percent, followed the program less faithfully, rating "Good to Fair" on at least two of the four areas; they enjoyed a 50 percent reduction in symptoms. The remainder of the patients, about 25 percent, performed "Poor to Fair" on all, but most of those who did anything benefited to some degree. (Some who performed poorly still greatly decreased their symptoms, as much as 60 percent, just by going through the program. Perhaps it can be explained by their heightened awareness, perhaps by their having taken responsibility for their lives.)

1,000 CASES
Percentage of Patients

	I 25%	II 50%	III 25%
Exercise	Good	Good to Fair	Poor to Fair
Nutrition	Good	on at least two	on all
Stress Reduction	Good		
Ecology	Good		
% Reduction in Symptoms (average)	90%	65%	Slight (30% average)

Each year, as the patients are rechecked, more of them will advance a level, into or toward Category I.

The moral is: Something is better than nothing, and tomorrow it may lead to something more.

The figures in the table are probably a reliable guide to what true preventive health care can accomplish. Contrast this chart, for example, with the rising morbidity, or sickness, rate in this country. With Human Life Styling, morbidity goes down; generally over the country, it's going up. In "health checkups" at most clinics today, nutrition, exercise and stress factors are not evaluated. The checkups amount to early detection only; the number of symptoms is virtually unchanged. The old sacred cow, traditional medicine's annual physical examination, is simply not relevant to health. The problem is that most physicians are excellent diagnosticians and treaters of disease but there just hasn't been a large group of physicians who could be consulted for health in the sense that we have been using the word in this book—the ratio is 200 to 1. Each patient needs primarily a health physician, who will help him stay well and refer him to competent disease-treaters if necessary. Instead of the present ratio, we need a trend to the reverse proportion.

Inevitably the question arises: Has Human Life Styling produced any negative results? No—not when the program was followed as directed in this book. There have been a few minor side effects when a patient "went overboard," seeking to change his life patterns overnight. A few patients have attempted to step up their aerobic program too fast and have suffered strained or pulled leg muscles. These could have been prevented by building up their exercise capacity gradually, as recommended. Diet improvement has been without any ill effects, although a few patients have turned up with stomach aches from taking too much vitamin C on an empty stomach. Here again the patient had forgotten a part of the advice or had overdone things; in another patient this might not have occurred, because of individual differences.

It is better for the schizophrenic *not* to meditate at first; this patient needs to remain in the realistic world until he is improved. All others can only benefit from this mode of reducing stress.

By concentrating on the specific problems of particular individuals, case histories tell much about the effectiveness

of Human Life Styling. In order to demonstrate the importance of full individual participation in the program, as well
as some of the problems encountered, we have included cases
representing various degrees of success. These range from
the "dropout" to the "stars."

The case of D.D. illustrates how an individual can reap
minimal or no gain from the program because of his own
limited participation in it.

D.D., thirty-five, was a classic victim of "spiral down." He
drank six beers and smoked two packs of cigarettes a day,
was obese, and was under constant stress at home but
wouldn't express himself and face his problems head-on. The
lab examination of his blood fats spelled out some of the
details of his problem: his cholesterol was an extremely elevated 400 milligrams percent and his triglycerides were 400
milligrams percent (100 is about normal for triglycerides).

If he went on a *very* low carbohydrate diet, with no beer,
and exercised, it was explained to him, he would feel good
and his triglycerides and cholesterol levels would drop to
almost normal. He was also counseled on how he might improve the problems in his home life.

Unhappily, even weekly visits to the office failed to stop
his compulsive bent toward overindulging, and an up-and-
down pattern developed. He wouldn't work on his psychological self-destructiveness and finally he stopped coming in.
D.D., in effect, became a dropout, though his risk of a
coronary was extremely high and his chance of living five
more years very low, based on statistics. (Four brothers and
a sister had had early coronaries.) Yet if he had continued
to work on himself he could have looked forward to a long
life.

Other patients have approached the program more positively than did D.D. but failed to embrace it totally. These,
as indicated in the chart, enjoy striking benefits, though they

are not at an optimal level of health. Most of these either perform "fair" on the total program or tend to ignore one of the three directly health-related sections. One such patient was P.H.

P.H., forty, was lovely, proper and compulsive. Tired and tense, she complained on her first visit of an aching neck.

She did marvelously on her nutrition. She soon changed over to a practically perfect diet. Slowly she began to work on her stress and face her home problems, while improving her attitudes. The difficulty with P.H. was that she hadn't started her aerobic exercise program, even when repeatedly reminded. "Sweating is unpleasant," she explained. Her attitude seemed to be "I feel good—why do the whole thing?" although it was explained to her that the program was for growth, encouraging the maximum that is possible for a patient. As she "loosens up" psychologically, she probably will enjoy exercise. That may take as much as five more years.

Then there are the stars of Human Life Styling, those who follow the program reasonably well and benefit accordingly. We believe the cases that follow may provide some insight into the inroads that preventive medicine could make into the tangled maze of pain, suffering and despair in this country—if it were a national way of life.

Our first two cases exemplify how health and degeneration are frequently family matters—not because of blood relationships but because of life styles.

J.Y., a fifty-year-old schoolteacher, had suffered a progressively worsening arthritis for the past twenty years. Now he used a cane and was in constant pain. For four years he had experienced severe soreness in his tongue and he had lung "crackles," frequent colds and respiratory infections. (A lung crackle, heard through the stethoscope, indicates loose mucus or some other abnormality in the bronchi.) Recently he had complained of anxiety and fatigue.

At the time of his examination he had already been to ten different physicians for various complaints. He was very tense and trembled, and when the door opened he jumped. He seemed to drag himself into the examining room, where it was found that, among his other problems, he had irregular heartbeats.

Although he had been trying to improve his diet over the past few years, he had previously been a heavy sugar eater and was still consuming white starch. He ate almost no raw foods but was taking a few supplements.

He started gradually on the Human Life Styling program. He ate raw food at every meal and barred all empty calories. He began swimming and flexing exercises. He took high-potency multivitamins, with special attention to vitamin C, calcium and magnesium.

Within a year, almost all his symptoms were gone. He was having no colds at all. He was much calmer; his fatigue was gone and he was able to teach much more effectively. His arthritis was not gone, of course, but now he could walk without his cane much of the time. Although he was still swimming, he had to be reminded occasionally to resume his exercise program. His follow-up questionnaire indicated that 95 percent of his symptoms were gone.

B.Y., fifty-year-old schoolteacher and wife of J.Y., had had a severely sore tongue for years. She did not smoke. She had been to numerous physicians and one major nationally known clinic about her constant sore throat and cough, without relief. For years she had sustained a high degree of stress.

Like her husband, she was very nervous and appeared sick and fatigued. Her finger joints were painful, although she had been increasing her dietary supplements over the last few years. However, her supplements were not the appropriate ones for her; she ate few raw foods and did very little exercise.

Within a year of fairly faithful participation in the Human Life Styling program she was practically free of all her symptoms. Her tongue was no longer sore. She was not tired and was much calmer. Because she seemed to have certain symptoms of carbohydrate intolerance, she was placed on a low-carbohydrate diet with supplements. She was now swimming and doing her exercises regularly.

"I feel great!" she said. "I never felt this good before in my life. If only one doctor at that great clinic had simply taken a dietary and exercise history, I wouldn't have had to put up with this all these years."

S.T., thirty-nine, nervous, talkative and distraught, was in anguish on her first visit. Burdened with family problems, she had gained sixty pounds in four years. A two-pack-a-day smoker, she had chronic bronchitis, severe nasal pharyngitis, constant backache, frequent spells of nervousness, irritability, tiredness and "female trouble." A total wreck, in other words. She thought of her life as almost at an end.

Her glucose tolerance test, which measured her body's handling of this one sugar, resulted in a completely "flat" abnormal curve, indicating overresponse of insulin and some degree of carbohydrate intolerance.

Over the next year she embarked on a gradual weight-loss program. She stopped all empty calories and took supplements. She began exercising fairly regularly. Within a year her weight had not gone down sharply, because she was erratic on cutting her food intake, but most of her symptoms had left. She was now able to be a real person, with much less nervousness.

And she was planning to marry. She represented a complete change from the tired wreck initially seen. Because she was feeling so much better, she was making a new commitment to undertake a lifelong weight-control program.

W.B., forty-five, a thin and tired-looking man, complained primarily of insufficient sleep and numerous gastrointestinal symptoms, as well as recent shortness of breath. A very self-effacing kind of person, he was bent over so that he always looked at the ground.

W.B. had been a hard worker most of his life, and just in recent years had he begun to feel run-down and low. His seemed to be a classic case of the male change-of-life condition. Before his first visit he had made some attempt to exercise and to improve his diet. A computerized dietary survey, however, reported that he was still consuming the equivalent of twenty teaspoonfuls of sugar daily. His intake of empty calories was high. Though he denied it, he looked severely depressed.

Over the next year he gradually developed as a jogger until he was accumulating 30 aerobic points each week. He improved his diet diligently. A disciplined person by habit, he rigorously carried out his relaxation techniques. In addition to the other elements of Human Life Styling, he went through a humanistic growth therapy program, consisting of Gestalt therapy.

In one year his back was straight. He showed no sign of depression. He was an entirely confident, competent person. He now has his wife on the program and has encouraged many others. He had very effectively faced the world, simply by changing his life style.

M.G., thirty-five, was nothing short of a total pathetic wreck when she walked in the door. She had reached "the last straw." (It is beyond understanding why so many people have to be at death's door before they try some natural therapy!) She had suffered from severe asthma, bronchitis and frequent urinary infections for much of her life. Previously diagnosed as a borderline schizophrenic, she had been treated by a psychiatrist for years. She had been through a highly traumatic divorce and could not relate to her family at all. Her hair was stringy and she trembled constantly, as if to escape from her skin.

A brief mental test indicated some signs of schizophrenia, and a six-hour blood sugar, or glucose tolerance, test demonstrated abnormal drops at one-hour and five-hour points, with symptoms of hypoglycemia. Her diet was deplorable. She smoked and was taking no supplements. Her complaints seemed infinite—she checked almost every symptom on her health questionnaire. She was also considered anemic, with 12 grams of hemoglobin—although many physicians had told her that was not bad.

Once on the program, she stopped eating sweets, started taking niacin along with other vitamins in high dosages, and began eating raw vegetables and exercising. Her appearance was so remarkable the next time Dr. McCamy saw her that he had to refer to her chart to see who she was. Her hair was arranged gracefully. She was calm and smiling. Her lungs sounded much clearer, now that she had stopped smoking.

She said that as soon as she stopped eating sugar and started taking niacin, she immediately felt better, in one day, and had felt great since. She was eating six times a day, good, natural low-carbohydrate food in small snacks, and exercising daily. She was clinically improved in every way. She suddenly had a great deal of energy and, being an exceptionally bright person, she wanted to do in one month everything she had not been able to do for the previous ten years or more. Although this created a problem, she was instructed to direct her energy appropriately and do a little bit at a time.

G.Z., sixty, a professional with a very responsible position, came in only at the insistence of his wife, who had enjoyed very good results on her health program.

G.Z. complained of being tired though he said he had always felt good and had never really had anything wrong with him. However, an evaluation of his health habits turned up a poor dietary history, a heavy coffee intake and a history of smoking. His athletic schedule was very erratic. He worked in high school athletics during the season and felt really alive; then the rest of the year he did almost nothing and invariably gained around twenty pounds, so that every year his weight fluctuated by that amount. (This up-and-down weight pattern, so typical of the American way of life, is one of the most dangerous aspects of our culture.) His labs results were equally revealing, showing high blood pressure, a certain degree of chronic lung disease, a very high blood cholesterol and high triglycerides, with a Type IV hyperlipemia, which is a classification for the fats in the bloodstream. This placed him in a high risk category for a coronary.

G.Z. represents the typical patient who thinks he feels good and might have gone to a physician and been told, "You're in good shape," even though he was obese, had elevated blood fats and was tired. He might have been cautioned to watch his diet, with no dietary, exercise and stress evaluations ever made.

Instead he was told that he was in an extremely high risk group for a coronary: he could have one at any time. It was pointed out, however, that it was not inevitable that he have one; with a complete change in dietary and other habits he could modify his statistics in the direction of a long and happy life.

G.Z. chose to correct his health habits. He rapidly decreased his risk of coronary and started feeling much better. Once he improved his diet and began exercising the year round, his fatigue dropped. He took a more relaxed view of his job. He only needed to be instructed on his new health habits and periodically encouraged to follow them.

N.E., thirty-eight, a pleasant, successful business executive, had suffered from severe fatigue for a year. Although he also had frequent respiratory infections, upper gastrointestinal distress, chronic heartburn, nasal stuffiness and was obese, he had previously been told there was nothing seriously wrong. (People who are working hard accept low levels of health as normal.)

A total evaluation of his life contradicted that. His diet: ten cups of coffee and thirty teaspoonfuls of sugar per day, with bad eating habits. He had been under severe stress for four years in his job, working an eighteen-hour day. No exercise. His blood cholesterol was nearly 300, dangerously high as far as preventive medicine is concerned.

Even though no previous upper gastrointestinal test had shown an anatomical disease, it was obvious that the heartburn indicated something was wrong; cutting out coffee alone could have improved it. Thus, N.E. started eliminating empty calories, stopped drinking coffee and went on a weight-loss program of eating, basically, meats and vegetables. He was asked to schedule his life to include exercise.

Within six months his fatigue was greatly lessened. His weight was down and he had more zest. In the process he had dropped his risk of coronary from over 50 percent to about 20 percent. His work schedule was still excessive and far from being desirable, but he was taking steps to improve this over a long period of time. Meanwhile, he was working more effectively and delegating responsibilities.

Had he continued the way he was going, N.E. most likely would have dropped dead of a coronary in his forties or early fifties. Now he can look forward to perhaps forty or more years of good, healthy, active life, for he has no symptoms.

H.J., forty-five, was afflicted with organic disturbances that included a bent-over posture, depression, frequent nervous spells and stomach upsets, an ulcer in the past, kidney trouble and kidney stone.

A search for possible degenerative factors turned up a high sugar and junk-food intake, a very high consumption of coffee, the smoking of two packs of cigarettes a day. She had the outward appearance of being a rather heavy drinker, though she denied taking more than four drinks a day.

She started taking supplements and improved her diet with fresh vegetables and much raw food. She commenced a good walking program for her exercise.

Within several months she was vivacious, a really lively person, and able to handle her day-to-day work better. While her initial glucose tolerance test had recorded a very high blood sugar at one hour, followed by a subsequent abnormal drop, a repeat blood sugar test showed it to be normal. She was finally able to attack her smoking addiction and, at last, she admitted that she was an alcoholic and that she was now ready and able to stop her drinking. Now she has a whole new life in front of her.

L.M., forty-five, a professional, had experienced increasing fatigue and anxiety tension over the past few years. He had episodes of diarrhea as often as five to ten times a day. Intestinal gas was so severe that he couldn't even hold conferences. As he discussed his problems in the clinic, he constantly grimaced and made other abrupt facial expressions. He seemed unable to even narrate his story without moving jerkily almost every second. He talked through clenched teeth: a totally anxious, degenerating product of our modern culture. He was one of the most extremely tense individuals Dr. McCamy had ever seen.

L.M. had been under heavy business and professional stress for years as the result of certain reverses. He was drinking much coffee, which is often the major cause of intestinal distress, but he hadn't realized that eliminating coffee should be the first action for anyone with these problems. He was exercising not at all and his diet was deficient in many areas.

By this time he had had three different work-ups by internists at major medical centers. His diagnoses had been "irritable colon" and other vague disorders, but he had received no benefit.

Now he improved his diet, eliminated coffee, started taking in acidophilus bacteria from yogurt for intestinal health, plus supplements and digestive enzymes. Within one month the diarrhea was gone. He gradually increased his exercise, worked on the stress reduction and relaxation techniques, until he was a smiling, pleasant person. He sat still, his grimaces fading, and looked at you in a way one could never have imagined possible for him. He seemed to be taking life more in stride. His symptoms, which initially had numbered one hundred out of a possible three hundred, were down to four. He was at a plateau where he was constantly improving himself.

A further work-up that included hair analysis, a newer therapy, demonstrated abnormal ratios of minerals, particularly lead. He also had arteriosclerotic plaques in his aorta, a high risk factor in coronary. For these conditions he was referred to another clinic for chelation therapy, a procedure that removes lead and extra calcium deposits. In addition, he was placed on megavitamin therapy—the administration of certain vitamins in massive doses. He exhibited further improvement.

In L.M.'s case, biofeedback therapy was used in conjunction with Human Life Styling. This form of operant conditioning involved the insertion of needles into his scalp to help him relearn habit patterns so as not to tense up his scalp or muscles when he felt stress. Electrodes were attached to the tensed area. When the muscle became taut, a red light would flash and a beep would sound. By trying to prevent the light and sound, he was able to subdue the nervous tic. This form of biofeedback therapy has proved to be successful for tension headaches, facial grimaces, grinding of teeth, dermatitis scratching, tapping of feet and other subconscious tensing patterns that people tend to adopt readily when they are under stress. There are also biofeedback mechanisms that help the person reduce his blood pressure, by responding to the machine's indicator. Other biofeedback techniques enable one to move into the alpha state more easily.

The difficulty of some of these exotic techniques is, as it was with L.M., that the person tends to use the exotic equipment—at no small cost—and forget about the basic problem. Busy professional people, especially, have to be reminded about exercising and diet. Some of them may forget to give precedence to building up the body and mind so that they function naturally and responsibly.

R.R., thirty-four, a recent divorcee, previously diagnosed as schizophrenic, had behind her four psychiatric hospital admissions, with almost no benefit. She had additionally been to two major clinics for frequent medical treatment. She felt "strung out" and constantly tired. As a result of her highly nervous state she had been unable to maintain her marriage and now, although she had been very secure financially, she was trying to work as a waitress.

Her diet was almost totally unsatisfactory, she was not exercising, she was taking no supplements, and she had a deleterious pattern of stress in her past.

Within one week on the Human Life Styling program, she exhibited such rapid improvement that Dr. McCamy is still amazed. After a week with no sugar at all (in her case, because of hypoglycemia, no carbohydrates at first), but with high doses of niacin, regular multivitamins, daily exercise, six small meals a day consisting of a high percentage of raw foods and no processed foods, she was smiling and outgoing, much, much advanced. Two weeks after she began she had a regular male friend and exuberantly proclaimed, "Life is great!"

At no time in her life had she ever felt this good. Yet it had simply involved a change in her dietary and exercise habits. Her reaction was one of constant amazement. "*Why* didn't someone mention this to me before?"

Which was her doctor's exact thought.

K.L., an attractive forty-year-old woman, came in after nearly lifelong therapy for depression. Over the last year her depression had worsened; she was becoming deranged in her thinking and could not concentrate at all. She had no confidence in herself. She was now experiencing some dizziness and had many vague symptoms, as well as frequent headaches and recurrent bladder infections. Though her main affect was depression, on her questionnaire she listed twenty different abdominal complaints and over forty nervous symptoms.

In other words, she was a presuicidal, nonfunctioning human being.

She had been to numerous doctors and they had diagnosed depression. She was prescribed frequent antidepressants and other drugs. Her condition kept deteriorating, even though the laboratory indicated no particular major problems.

As the three major factors of illness were evaluated, however, her medical condition could be seen in an entirely new light. She was consuming thirty teaspoonfuls of sugar daily. Her diet was deficient in fifteen different factors. Her exercise was negative. Her stress response had been very high all her life; she had rarely been free from stress. In addition to all this, she was drinking twelve cups of coffee a day and smoking two packs of cigarettes.

Within one month of simply taking walks, improving the nutrient value of her diet and practicing some relaxation techniques, she had decreased her medications and was beginning to think more clearly. She was starting, she said, to feel like a human being.

A year later she was an alert, active, healthy-looking person, who smiled easily and lived an effective life. She had stopped smoking, no longer drank coffee, ate a good balanced diet, was getting in 30 aerobic points a week, was doing relaxation techniques and was taking life in stride. Her nervous symptoms had declined from over forty to a meager three.

She had said Yes to life with body and soul, and now she was reaping the rewards.

In the cases of some of these patients it would have been very easy to give a final diagnosis such as depression, menopause, chronic fatigue or other psychiatric labels. The true diagnoses are almost always malnutrition, lack of exercise and chronic stress reaction. If a person is hospitalized with pneumonia, the diagnosis on the hospital chart will read "pneumonia." But the true cause most often is malnutrition, which leads to the lowering of resistance factors so that one is susceptible to disease and contracts pneumonia. Doctors work too late in the disease-resistance cycle to recognize this.

Many persons have been able to change their approach to living merely as the result of a few simple suggestions about their way of looking at life. Very often one never knows whether it's the changing of mental sets or the diet and exercise that produce the new outlook. All we know is that the whole program works. Why worry over which does what?

The payoff is to start seeing changes in yourself and to learn to know yourself. Many a person has not realized what a remarkable person he or she has inside. Once a person's health habits become an integral part of his life, a whole new plateau opens up. Then one sees that there's no limit to how far one can go toward self-realization.

8

To Renew a Nation

A heart transplant is an exotic scientific event. It is a quick answer, the immediate swapping of a diseased, worn-out heart for a healthy one, and a new start, handed the passive patient by the miracle-makers of medical science.

The glamorous heart transplant has also been one of the most massive concentrations of scientific and medical effort that the world has ever seen. It may require the total services of twenty-eight nurses, thoracic surgeons and other highly trained technicians. As much as fifty units of blood may be needed. The cost for one heart transplant may reach as high as $50,000 or more. (A coronary bypass operation costs an average of $8,000 each.) On the ecological side, it is a challenge to compute the amount of energy used in this single operation.

There is just one hitch. The facts show that patients waiting in line for heart transplants live longer than those who have the operation.

With a very brief investment in time every day, these same patients could have prevented their heart disease, provided it was not of the congenital type. The program of preventive medicine in this book can do it. The road to a heart transplant or cancer surgery or intensive stroke care is a dead-end spiral. It doesn't matter what exotic scientific techniques await us at the end of the spiral; it's no fun getting there. The heart transplant is an example of an ecologically nonworkable system. We don't have the resources to provide everyone with a transplant—even if it worked. The way of preventive medicine is more promising, and we can all afford it.

It's typical of our culture not only to want to know but to know why. Perhaps this is one explanation of the popular worship of the heart transplant and the lesser interest in preventive medicine. But if something works, and is safe, why wait to find out *how* it works before using it?

The need today is obviously great for disease-treatment doctors, and they will always be needed. In fact, they are so swamped today by patients that they cannot keep pace with our exponentially rising rate of illness. We believe that the only way this nation can become healthy and survive is by changing our life style. It must be carried out on an individual basis, for each of us is responsible, ultimately, for his or her own health. But it must also become a national way of life or we will continue to spiral down, while medical costs and physical degeneration spiral upward.

Political Leaders

Our political leadership will play a large role in determining the kind of medical system we will have in the coming years. Will it be prevention-oriented, or a massive attempt to continue disease treatment? Certainly prepaid systems, in which the subscriber pays a flat fee and is entitled to basic health-care services, generally can be made preventive more easily, but whatever system is used, we must add risk-factor testing and preventive programs to have *any* effect on raising the level of general health.

It makes no difference whether we have a national health system, to which everyone, including the poorest, has access, or a preferred health plan, as long as it is disease-treatment-oriented. With either one, there will be no decrease in mortality or morbidity. Disease treatment, we can't say too many times, will not keep disease from occurring. If we do not become prevention-oriented in our health-delivery plans, we will eventually reach a budgetary and health crisis, no matter whose plan it is. The fundamental question that our statesmen must answer is: Do you want people well or do you want ever-spiraling disease-treatment costs? The right answer could save the country $45 billion and God knows how much pain and sorrow.

The answer to that question will not come from the roots of any specific ideology, Left, Right or Middle, but from a concern for people. No nation with failing health can be great.

Patients

While we wait for our medical and political establishments to move toward prevention, we as individuals can begin putting our own health in order. By changing our own life styles we can influence others by our examples. Patients can have considerable influence on their doctors. Don't let anyone take out your organs or administer drugs to you without explaining the side effects. It's your body and your right to know. Don't be afraid to ask your doctor if he is in health care, as did the student at the beginning of this book. If he isn't interested in prevention, there's no reason to criticize him; he hasn't been trained for it. Show this book to your doctor. It's important for each of you to know where the other stands. If you have a good, trusted disease-treater, you still, we hope, would use a health physician trained in these techniques.

For individuals who are following Human Life Styling's precepts on your own, it's important to keep a written record of your progress and goals. You have to review it periodically, preferably monthly, but at least every six months or once a year. Repeat, repeat, repeat until the new habits are established.

Doctors

The physician who is interested in instituting more preventive techniques in his practice can set his own pace. He can begin on a modest scale, by selecting as few as ten of his patients. Once he gets started, he can gradually include more and more patients. Today's doctors are highly qualified at disease treatment, but it is very difficult for one to keep up with the disease field, such as the ramifications of heart disease, plus the techniques of disease prevention, such as may be found in the nutritional literature. Most doctors have never asked a patient to write down a diet survey that would provide an overall view of what the patient was specifically eating.

Since disease can be prevented and patients can take responsibility for their health, if advised, then why not emphasize this? If your patients then get sick, let them know that they have made themselves sick. Look upon illness as a *breakdown* in your health care plan, not as a place to start therapy.

If, however, you choose to be only a disease diagnostician and treater, then clearly and honestly tell your patients this. Many physicians will prefer this role. You will continue to have an important place in total health care, though not as a total health advisor.

We as physicians must realize and admit that we were not trained in *health* techniques. The choice, then, for traditional physicians is 1) to learn health medicine and be a total health care person or 2) let other professionals do it. But choose we must.

Setting Up a Preventive Program

The tools that a physician needs are few: a seven-day diet sheet on which the patient writes down exactly what he eats at every meal for a week, and an exercise survey. The nurse can check these, to save the physician's time. Then a stress analysis needs to be made. About thirty questions would suffice. There are such questionnaires available, or the doctor can work up his own. Is the patient's sex life adequate? Did he have a happy or miserable childhood? Is life satisfactory now? (An unenthusiastic "Okay" should be clue enough that it isn't.) How are things at home? At work? This could be followed by physical questions relating to stress.

These analyses, which provide a more thorough review of the total person and his risk factors, can be done with no waste of time. The physician can glance at the diet sheet and learn much. By making a few suggestions for specific substitutions, he can encourage the patient to improve. For instance: "Did you eat any sugar?" "No," replies the patient. "Fine," says the doctor. "Well, I see this soda cracker here. Next time you could substitute whole-grain bread for that." The diet sheets streamline the operation and at the same time help the patient to be more aware of his eating habits. Each visit should begin with the patient handing in a seven-day diet list. On the first visit, a computerized total nutritional survey is recommended.

Exercise can be analyzed on the same sheet. All that is necessary is to check the number of points and see that there is gradual improvement. If the patient drops down in points, remind him to work his way back up.

It may require some practice to teach relaxation techniques. In Dr. McCamy's clinic, these techniques are taught during three group visits in which the patients practice together. Sessions can be held at night once a month, with perhaps twenty or thirty participating at a nominal fee. Sometimes a confident assistant can conduct the relaxation sessions.

Although he's not God, the doctor remains a very important figure to the patient. If the patient is made a partner in achieving and maintaining health, that relationship becomes even more vital.

This partnership should begin by the doctor's taking the patient into his confidence right away, explaining the meaning of all his lab work and the physical examination. What significance does each finding have for the patient's present and future health? What can he do about it to achieve and maintain health? He can give the patient an approximate percentage risk for his most likely illness, especially coronary thrombosis.

The patient's life can be changed merely by the physician's getting over to him the view: *It's not what I can do for you, it's what you can do for yourself.* As the patient is given immediate responsibility, the partnership in health begins.

The doctor is most effective when he teaches his patients to teach. It is not enough to tell them that sugar is bad. They must know why. Otherwise someone else will think of them, "Is he some kind of nut? What's wrong with eating sugar?" That intimidates people. But if they have the medical reasons for it, showing that sugar has no food value, is absorbed too quickly and robs the body to metabolize itself, they have a ready answer for their friends. We don't recommend that anyone become a "health food nut"—just that they eat real food. Teen-age patients present great difficulties. If handled properly, and with luck, the doctor can build up their confidence and they, in turn, can change many in their peer group.

Dentists

This is a particularly good time for dentists to make a profound impact on the nation's health, perhaps even more so than physicians. It is relatively simple to have the patient fill out exercise and diet sheets. It would be helping the entire body as well as the teeth; it's a matter of considering the mouth a part of the whole body.

A cavity is a failure of the dental health system, not the place to start. Gum and tooth diseases are totally preventable through local cleaning practices *and nutrition.* Stress can also be a factor. If a dentist stops his patients from eating sugar, he can do more than a physician might do in restoring health.

Dentists may use the techniques of predictive dentistry, advising the patient, "If you don't follow a specific preventive program, you're likely to lose your teeth in ten years." Then the patient has something tangible to work with, in order to cut his risk down, just as he would with heart disease.

Psychologists

Psychologists, psychiatrists and those in allied sciences can just as easily apply these principles. If the goal is truly to help people get well, then why not try what works? During a visit from a client or patient, it takes only a few minutes to recommend exercise and dietary improvement. Esalen Institute, for one, has already started teaching Human Life Styling training, and more such training sessions for the helping professions are expected in the future.

Clergymen

Clergymen of all faiths have a remarkable opportunity. The striving for health is not a fiefdom for one profession only; it is the concern of all of us. If a clergyman's job is to uplift people and guide them to be in touch with God as they know him or to be a part of God, then the development of that person in all his aspects is a logical goal. There is no reason why church meals can't substitute fresh fruit and decaffeinated coffee for apple pie and coffee. It may be that more God-awareness and alpha-state sessions, with less verbalizing, will help more people *know* the cosmic power, rather than know *about* it. A clergyman could start his own Human Life Styling groups, to help people build their body temples.

Toward a National Life Style

There is no area of our national life that should be omitted from our working toward a new life style. Companies encouraging or organizing Human Life Styling sessions would benefit through having happier, more efficient employees. Small businessmen would experience better work production personally and from their employees. Manufacturers could provide much-needed leadership now by producing worthwhile food. Labor unions could establish clinics for preventive medicine, or could set them up jointly with management. Most of all, our next generations hold the key to our future. Our children must start eating better, exercising more, living less stressed lives and learning how to treat our environment better than we have done. Teachers and all who work with children, especially parents, have a rare opportunity to make personal impacts for health and, probably, survival.

There is a vacuum in health care now. Only a few, perhaps a few hundred, are actively teaching true health care in this country. We need to start redistributing medical training funds, in order to provide more true health training. We need fewer persons trained in disease treatment and more in preventive medicine, until there is at least a fifty-fifty balance.

It is also hoped that each of our large clinics in this country will add a preventive medicine section. This would enable each patient to have not only an excellent disease work-up but also competent dietary, exercise and stress evaluations. These could be explained to the patient, with his risk factors spelled out clearly—compared to the normal, not the average. Total-health centers are needed, so that people can go and learn total-health living and doctors can be trained there to teach it, as will be done at Esalen.

As a profession, dentists are far ahead of physicians in preventive techniques. Almost any profession could train its members in the principles of Human Life Styling. Physicians could add to their own programs. Paramedical Human Life Stylers can be trained, since a medical license is not necessary to prescribe vitamins and diet or recommend exercise and stress reduction techniques. Initially a doctor could examine the patient to confirm that he is free of serious illness. Almost anyone could do what Dr. McCamy has been doing in his own office. With a year or two of training behind him, a college student should be able to open an office as a Human Life Styler.

Or perhaps, since the death rate can be expected to decline, putting a great many morticians out of work, the logical move would be to train them as Human Life Stylers!

In the meantime we can all do a great deal. Starting a jogging club could do more good for the health of your community than all the medical treatment it is now receiving. Start now, eating well, exercising, reducing your stress response and caring for your environment. Remember you are on a lifelong program. Be healthy yourself, so that your children will be healthy, and your grandchildren after them.

It is a very exciting time in which to live. Spread the word. See that two other persons start practicing Human Life Styling. Ask each to recruit two others. Keep it simple. Keep it going. And let it grow.

Exponentially.

Appendix I

A DIRECTORY OF PREVENTION-ORIENTED ORGANIZATIONS

Center for Human Life Styling
P.O. Box 6585, St. Petersburg Beach, Florida 33736

International Academy of Preventive Medicine
and Ortho-molecular Medicine
624 Shartle Circle, Houston, Texas 77024

Southern Academy of Clinical Nutrition
308 North Taylor Street, Goldsboro, North Carolina 27530

Price-Pottenger Foundation
Granville Knight, M.D.
2901 Wilshire Boulevard, Suite 345, Santa Monica, California 90403

International Academy of Metabology, Inc.
2236 Suree Ellen Lane, Altadena, California 91001

Esalen Institute
Big Sur, California 93920

Academy of Parapsychology and Medicine
314 Second Street, Los Altos, California 94022

Association for Humanistic Psychology
416 Hoffman, San Francisco, California 94114

Natural Foods Association
P.O. Box 210, Atlanta, Texas 75551

Wilderness Report, The Wilderness Society
1901 Pennsylvania Avenue NW, Washington, D.C. 20006

National Audubon Society
    950 Third Avenue, New York, New York 10022

Planned Parenthood/World Population
    515 Madison Avenue, New York, New York 10022

Friends of the Earth
    30 East 42 Street, New York, New York 10017
    529 Commercial Street, San Francisco, California 94111
    917 15th Street NW, Washington, D.C. 20005
    1372 Kapiolani Boulevard, Honolulu, Hawaii 96814
    P.O. Box 1977, Anchorage, Alaska 99501

Center for Science in the Public Interest
    1779 Church Street NW, Washington, D.C. 20036

American Medical Association
Division of Preventive Medicine
    535 North Dearborn Street, Chicago, Illinois 60610

American Society of Prospective Medicine
    Methodist Hospital, Indianapolis, Indiana

National Health Federation
    212 West Foothills Boulevard, Monrovia, California 91016

American College of Preventive Medicine
    801 Old Lancaster Road, Bryn Mawr, Pennsylvania 19010

Gardens for All
    Charlotte, Vermont 05445

Alternative therapies may be helpful to some. Below are a few addresses to which you may write:

Chelation	American Academy of Medical Preventics
	350 Parnassus, Suite 700, San Francisco, California 94117
Rolfing	Guild for Structural Integration
	P.O. Box 1868, Boulder, Colorado 80302
Fasting	Bircher-Benner
	Kelterstrasse 48, CH 8044, Zurich, Switzerland
Acupuncture	American Acupuncture Research
	505 Park Avenue, Suite 1508, New York, New York 10022

Appendix II

SEVEN-DAY HEALTH DIARY

	BREAKFAST	LUNCH	DINNER
1st day			
2nd day			
3rd day			
4th day			
5th day			
6th day			
7th day			

Keep a record of all foods eaten for meals and snacks.
Record all sauces, sweeteners, spreads, syrups, types of bread, drinks, etc.
Record all exercise and amount of time spent relaxing.

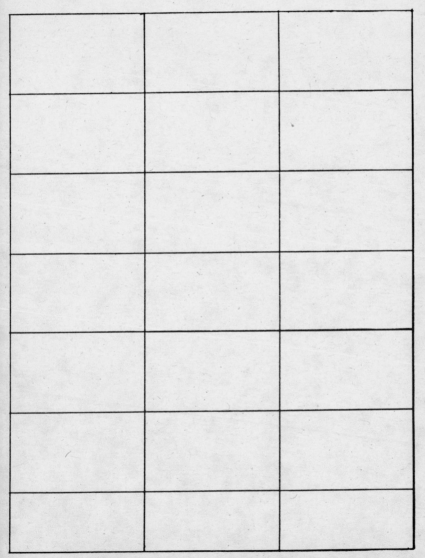

SNACKS	EXERCISE	RELAXATION

This simple sheet is the mainstay of any preventive program. Use it regularly.

An Essay on Sources

Footnotes have been eliminated from the text in the interest of increased readability. For those who wish to pursue these topics in more detail, the following bibliographic essay is broken down by pertinent chapters.

1. *The Concept of Human Life Styling*

The Larry Malone "experiment" was conducted by members of the Southern Academy of Clinical Nutrition. The Cheraskin-Ringsdorf quote is from their *Predictive Medicine: A Study in Strategy* (Mountain View, Calif.: Pacific Press Publishing Association, 1973), p. 1.

The HEW report on male life expectancy dropping from 1960 to 1970 was in *Medical Tribune*.

A helpful source for statistics on rising medical costs is Cheraskin and Ringsdorf's *New Hope for Incurable Diseases* (New York: Exposition Press, 1971), chap. 1. Their *Predictive Medicine*, pp. 61–72, provides a concept of normal versus average values; pp. 34–44, the gradation concept of disease development; pp. 25–33, the host resistance-susceptibility factors. More on rising medical costs can be seen in "The Staggering Cost of Applying our Knowledge," *Medical World News*, June 2, 1972, pp. 39–46.

2. *The Four Horsemen of Health*

Helpful sources for the compilation of the coronary proneness profile include Cheraskin and Ringsdorf, *Predictive Medicine,* pp. 8–16; Cheraskin, Ringsdorf, A. T. S. H. Setyaadmadja and R. A. Barrett, "Effect of Carbohydrate Supplements upon the Height of the T Wave in Lead I," *Angiology,* vol. 19, No. 4 (April 1968), pp. 225–31; S. L. Malhotra, "Dietary Factors and Ischemic Heart Disease," *American Journal of Clinical Nutrition,* October 20, 1971, pp. 1195–98.

Literature on heart disease has risen exponentially in the last few decades, so that any listing of material that we have examined would necessarily be selective. The famous Framingham studies are a basic beginning for any study of coronary heart disease. See William B. Kannel, "The Disease of Living," *Nutrition Today,* May/June, 1971, pp. 2–11. A recent follow-up on Framingham by Dr. Kannel was reported in "Heart Disease Risk Tests Formulated," *CD,* December 1973, p. 4. A study in progress that includes preventive modalities is Glenn M. Friedman, "Atherosclerosis and the Pediatrician," a program in Scottsdale, Arizona, which was presented in a paper before the American Public Health Association, November 1973.

A further sampling would include William B. Kannel and William P. Castelli, "The Framingham Study of Coronary Disease in Women," *Medical Times* 100, no. 5 (May, 1972), pp. 173–95; "Twenty Years After: Scientists Take Another Look at Framingham," *Doctors' Club Journal* 3, no. 1, pp. 34 ff.; "Arteriosclerosis: A Survey," *MD,* March 1972, pp. 79 ff.; "Heart Disease Survey 'Profiles' Death Risks," *Chronic Disease Management,* January 1973, pp. 1, 22–23; "When Irish Hearts Are Tested . . ." *Roche Image of Medicine and Research* 14, no. 2 (March 1972), p. 30; Tores Theorell et al., "A Longitudinal Study of 21 Subjects with Coronary Heart Disease: Life Changes, Catecholamine Excretion and Related Biochemical Reactions," *Psychosomatic Medicine,* November/December 1972, pp. 505–16; Jean Tache, "How Potassium and Exercise Work Together to Help Protect Your Heart," *Executive Health* 9, no. 9 (1973); Marguerite Gilbert Fowler, "Relationship of Serum Uric Acid to Achievement Motivation," *Psychosomatic Medicine* 35, no. 1 (January–February 1973), pp. 13–22; "Heart Disease Survey 'Profiles' Death Risks," *Chronic Disease Management,* January 1973, pp. 1 ff.

The effect of stress in heart disease is discussed popularly in Walter

McQuade, "What Stress Can Do to You," *Reader's Digest*, April 1972, pp. 111–14, and technically in Meyer Friedman et al., "Coronary-Prone Individuals (Type A Behavior Pattern): Growth Hormone Responses," *Journal of the American Medical Association*, August 16, 1971, pp. 929–32.

Blood pressure as a factor in stroke is assessed in William B. Kannel et al., "Epidemiologic Assessment of the Role of Blood Pressure in Stroke—The Framingham Study," JAMA, October 12, 1970, pp. 301–10. "Personality Characteristics of Stroke Victims," *Modern Medicine*, October 4, 1971, explores the factor of emotional stress.

Another article on hypertension is I. Pilowsky, D. Spalding, J. Shaw and P. I. Korner, "Hypertension and Personality," *Psychosomatic Medicine* 35, no. 1 (January–February 1973), pp. 50–56.

A recent report on control of stroke risk factors was given by Drs. Stanley C. Leonberg, Jr., and Frank A. Elliott to the American Medical Association, June 1973, as noted in "Reducing Stroke Mortality," *American Family Physician*, November 1973, p. 193. At the same meeting, Dr. Edward D. Freis demonstrated that a lowering of blood pressure resulted in a reduction of major complications.

On stroke, also see "Transient Ischemic Attacks and Hypertension Are Called Focal Points in Stroke Prevention," *Chronic Disease Management* 7, no. 1 (January 1973), p. 20, and "Stresses, Prevention, Aftercare, and Education," *ibid.*, p. 3.

The material on scrotal cancer among chimney sweeps and the risk factors in cervical cancer is from "Cervix Cancer—A Venereal Type Disease," a paper of the Cancer Control Center, North Hollywood, Calif., undated. Sources for a cancer proneness profile include Cheraskin and Ringsdorf, *Predictive Medicine*, pp. 16–23; Cheraskin and Ringsdorf, "Carbohydrate Metabolism and Carcinomatosis," *Cancer* 17, no. 2 (February 1964), pp. 159–62; Cheraskin, Ringsdorf, Setyaadmadja, Barrett, Aspray and Curry, "Cancer Proneness Profile: A Study in Weight and Blood Glucose," *Geriatrics* 23, no. 4 (April 1968), pp. 134–37; Cheraskin, Ringsdorf and Aspray, "Cancer Proneness Profile: A Study in Ponderal Index and Blood Glucose," *Geriatrics* 24, no. 8 (August 1969), pp. 121–25.

Risk factors in cancer of the esophagus are delineated in Philip Rubin et al., "Cancer of the Gastrointestinal Tract," *Journal of the American Medical Association* 226, no. 13 (December 24–31, 1973), pp. 1544–48. For insight into the relationship between refined carbohydrates and colon cancer, see interview with Denis P. Burkitt, "Western Civilization, Diet, and Disease," *Drug Therapy,* January 1974, pp. 51 ff.

Several aspects of food ingestion and cancer are discussed in J. H. Weisburger and Elizabeth K. Weisburger, "Food Additives and Chemical Carcinogens: On the Concept of Zero Tolerance," *Fd. Cosmet. Toxicol.* 6 (1968), pp. 235–42; Julian Aleksandrowioz et al., "Leuko- and Oncogenesis in the Light of Studies on the Metabolism of Magnesium and Its Turnover in Biocenosis," *Acta Medica Polona* 11, no. 4 (1970), pp. 289–302; and F. Homburger and Eliahu Boger, "The Carcinogenicity of Essential Oils, Flavors, and Spices: A Review," *Cancer Research,* November 1968, pp. 2372–74.

Emotional factors in cancer are discussed in David M. Kissen, "The Present Status of Psychosomatic Cancer Research," *Geriatrics,* January 1969, pp. 129–37, and Chester M. Southam, "Emotions, Immunology, and Cancer: How Might the Psyche Influence Neoplasia?" *Annals of the New York Academy of Sciences,* 164, art. 2 (October 14, 1969), pp. 473–75.

Discussion of life styles and preventive approaches include John S. Spratt, Jr., "Your Behavior and Cancer," draft manuscript, March 17, 1972, Cancer Research Center, Columbia, Mo., and John A. H. Lee, "Prevention of Cancer," *Postgraduate Medicine,* January 1972, pp. 84–88.

Hans Selye's now classic discovery of the General Adaptation Syndrome is presented in his book *The Stress of Life* (New York: McGraw-Hill, 1956).

On the effects of stress, also see Myron A. Hofer, Carl T. Wolff, Stanford B. Friedman and John W. Mason, "A Psychoendocrine Study of Bereavement: Part II. Observations on the Process of Mourning in Relation to Adrenocortical Function," *Psychosomatic Medicine* 34, no. 6 (November–December 1972), pp. 492–504.

The Eskimos' losses from the white man's ways are shown in Otto Schaefer, "When the Eskimo Comes to Town," *Nutrition Today,* November 10, 1971, pp. 8–16. A recent report on the Eskimo's present-day tendency toward glucose intolerance is George J. Mouratoff and Edward M. Scott, "Diabetes Mellitus in Eskimos After a Decade," *Journal of the American Medical Association* 226, no. 11 (December 10, 1973), pp. 1345–46.

Lewis C. Robbins and Jack H. Hall, *How to Practice Prospective Medicine* (Indianapolis: Slaymaker Enterprises, 1970) provides statistical data on risk factors pertaining to various diseases in different age groups. Exceedingly helpful, it is based on the death rate rather than degeneration.

A roundup of predictive, preventive methods is presented in "Physicians Can Detect Clues That Indicate Chance of an Illness," *Wall Street Journal*, November 8, 1972, p. 1. Another preventive view is D. P. Burkitt, "Are Our Commonest Killing Diseases Preventable?" *Rev. Europ. Études Clin. et Biol.* 15 (1970), pp. 253–54.

Increased risk of disease for overweight persons is shown in Alfred A. Rimm et al., "Disease and Obesity in 73,532 Women," *Obesity/Bariatric Medicine* 1, no. 4 (1972), pp. 77–87.

An additional profile is Cheraskin and Ringsdorf, "The Mental Illness Proneness Profile," *Alabama Journal of Medical Science* 10, no. 1 (January 1973), pp. 32–45.

3. *Ecological You*

The literature on ecology has proliferated and it should not be difficult to find enough books on the subject to satisfy the most curious person. Both inspiration and data for this chapter came, to a large extent, from two books: Donella H. Meadows, Dennis L. Meadows, Jorgen Randers and William W. Behrens III, *The Limits to Growth: A Report for the Club of Rome's Project on the Predicament of Mankind* (New York: Universe Books, 1972; paperback, New American Library) and G. Tyler Miller, Jr., *Replenish the Earth: A Primer in Human Ecology* (Belmont, Calif.: Wadsworth Publishing, 1972). Anyone wishing to learn hurriedly and well about our environmental problems could do so by reading these two books.

The J-curve concept comes from both books, although this particular depiction is from *Replenish the Earth*, which also contributed the simplified food chain example and the comparative impacts of the affluent and the poor upon the environment.

The Asimov quote on the population crisis is from his book *The Stars in Their Courses* (New York: Ace Books, 1972), p. 206.

The Club of Rome projections and recommendations in the last section of the chapter are from *The Limits to Growth*. A dissenting view is reported in "Delaying Doomsday," *Time*, October 15, 1973, p. 107.

An excellent recent work on energy resources and exponential growth is M. King Hubbert, "Survey of World Energy Resources," *Canadian Mining and Metallurgical Bulletin*, July 1973, pp. 1–17.

A pertinent book today, with the rising interest in nuclear power as an energy source, is Richard Curtis and Elizabeth Hogan, *Perils of the Peaceful Atom: The Myth of Safe Nuclear Power Plants* (New York: Ballantine Books, 1970).

If you are interested in a guide for ecological action, there is *Ecotactics: The Sierra Club Handbook for Environmental Activists* (New York: Pocket Books, 1970).

Some of the insecticide problems are discussed in Fred H. T. Schirley, "Pesticides: Relation to Environmental Quality," *Journal of the American Medical Association* 224, no. 8 (May 21, 1973), pp. 1157–59.

4. *Nutrition—Keeping It Simple*

Dr. Weston A. Price's studies are extracted from his *Nutrition and Physical Degeneration: A Comparison of Primitive and Modern Diets and Their Effects* (Santa Monica, Calif.: Price-Pottenger Foundation, 1945). It would be difficult to overpraise this excellent work. Anyone who is less than totally convinced of the vital link between poor nutrition and degenerative disease is advised to read it.

A study of diet and IQ in childhood is noted in "Effect on Intellect of Child's Malnutrition Held Reversible," *Family Practice News* 3, no. 17, p. 3.

Documentation of nutrition's role generally and especially during pregnancy can be found in Roger J. Williams, *Nutrition Against Disease: Environmental Prevention* (New York: Pitman Publishing, 1971). Another well-documented work is E. Cheraskin, W. M. Ringsdorf, Jr., and J. W. Clark, *Diet and Disease* (Emmaus, Pa.: Rodale Books, 1968). Other worthwhile sources include Adelle Davis's *Let's Eat Right to Keep Fit* and *Let's Cook It Right* (New York: Harcourt Brace Jovanovich, 1970 and 1962); Catharyn Elwood, *Feel Like a Million!* (New York: Devin-Adair, 1956); Joe D. Nichols and James Presley, *"Please, Doctor, Do Something!"* (Atlanta, Tex.: Natural Food Associates, 1972); George Watson, *Nutrition and Your Mind: The Psychochemical Response* (New York: Harper & Row, 1972); Melvin E. Page, *Degeneration-Regeneration* (St. Petersburg Beach, Fla.: Nutritional Development, 1949); Frances Moore Lappe, *Diet for a Small Planet* (New York: Friends of the Earth/Ballantine Books, 1971); Linda Clark, *Stay Young Longer: How to Add Years of Enjoyment to Your Life* (New York: Devin-Adair, 1961; paperback, Pyramid Books, 1968). Of particular value to dentists is Abraham E. Nizel, *Nutrition in Preventive Dentistry: Science and Practice* (Philadelphia: W. B. Saunders, 1972).

Primarily, our concept of the section on refined carbohydrates is that of T. L. Cleave, G. D. Campbell and N. S. Painter, *Diabetes, Coronary Thrombosis, and the Saccharine Disease,* 2d ed. (Bristol, England: John Wright & Sons, 1969). John Yudkin, *Sweet and Dangerous* (New York: Peter H. Wyden, 1972) further builds the case against sugar. A recent report of the Yemenite immigrants is in Gil Sedan, "Israeli Scientist Proves the Case Against Sugar," *Let's Live,* August 1973, pp. 104 ff.

Several books about specific vitamins that have proved helpful include Linus Pauling, *Vitamin C and the Common Cold* (San Francisco: W. H. Freeman, 1970); Irwin Stone, *The Healing Factor: "Vitamin C" Against Disease* (New York: Grosset & Dunlap, 1972); John M. Ellis and James Presley, *Vitamin B₆: The Doctor's Report* (New York: Harper & Row, 1973); and Wilfred E. Shute with Harald J. Taub, *Vitamin E for Ailing and Healthy Hearts* (New York: Pyramid House, 1970). The Stone book explores a large number of diseases in which vitamin C may play a healing role. The Ellis-Presley book establishes a number of relationships between vitamin B_6 deficiency and disease disorders, including rheumatism and arthritis, hormonal imbalances of pregnancy, menopause and the birth control pill, heart disease and diabetes. A detailed clinical report on vitamin C therapy is Frederick R. Klenner, "Observations on the Dose and Administration of Ascorbic Acid When Employed Beyond the Range of a Vitamin in Human Pathology," *Journal of Applied Nutrition* 23, no. 3–4 (Winter 1971), pp. 61–68.

Of the wealth of valuable information that has come from the hearings of the Select Committee on Nutrition and Human Needs, United States Senate, chaired by Senator George McGovern, we might single out *To Save the Children: Nutritional Intervention Through Supplemental Feeding* (Washington, D.C.: U.S. Government Printing Office, 1974) and Part 7 of the hearings, on school nutrition programs (1973). The effects of prenatal and pediatric malnutrition are explored in "Malnutrition and Brain Development," *Roche Image of Medicine & Research,* undated; "Finds Multivitamins Help to Prevent Birth Defects," *Family Practice News,* October 1, 1973, p. 8; and "Carbohydrate Metabolism, Congenital Defects Linked" *Family Practice News,* November 1, 1973, p. 25; Tom Brewer's column in *Medical Tribune,* October 24, 1973; Myron Winick, "Nutrition and the Growing Fetus," *Obstetrics & Gynecology* 1972, pp. 47–49.

A detailed technical examination of blood fats can be found in Robert I. Levy et al., "Dietary and Drug Treatment of Primary Hyperlipoproteinemia," *Annals of Internal Medicine* 77, no. 2 (August 1972), pp. 267–94.

Proof of alcohol's impairment of cardiac function is given in L. Gould et al., "Cardiac Effects of Two Cocktails in Normal Man," *Chest* 63 (June 1973), pp. 943–47.

Malnutrition in the U.S. is reported in "Highlights from the Ten-State Nutrition Survey," *Nutrition Today*, July/August 1972, pp. 4–11.

A careful scholarly and perfectly damning examination of smoking, Alton Ochsner, "On the Bitter Truth About Tobacco," *Executive Health* 9, no. 12 (1973), documents the aging effect of smoking, as well as its relationship with heart disease and stroke, cancers and sudden death. "There is no such thing as a safe cigarette," this distinguished doctor concluded. Dangers to nonsmokers who breathe others' fumes are noted in "Personal Air Pollution," *MD* (March 1972), p. 82.

The improvement of cardiovascular symptoms through health lectures on nutrition is reported in Cheraskin and Ringsdorf, "Reported Cardiovascular Symptoms and Signs Before and After Dietary Counsel," *Alabama Journal of Medical Sciences* 9, no. 2 (April 1972), pp. 174–79.

Finally, one of the most comprehensive, regular sources of readable nutritional information is *Prevention,* the monthly magazine published by Rodale Press, Emmaus, Pennsylvania. It is, incidentally, well-named.

5. *Descendants of Hunters*

We are chiefly indebted to Kenneth H. Cooper's work for the concept in this chapter on exercise: *The New Aerobics* (New York: M. Evans, 1970); *Aerobics* (M. Evans, 1968); and Mildred Cooper and Kenneth H. Cooper, *Aerobics for Women* (M. Evans, 1972). The charts at the end of the section are from *The New Aerobics.*

The Administration on Aging has published an exercise guide for older persons, *The Fitness Challenge . . . in the Later Years* (Washington, D.C.: U.S. Government Printing Office, 1968).

Dr. Edgar Gordon's lecture at the Southern Academy of Clinical Nutrition meeting on September 29, 1973, was helpful in further documenting the beneficial effects of exercise as a factor in lowering blood lipids. The University of Southern California finding on exercise as a "miracle drug" was cited in Joseph Hrachovec, *Keeping Young and Living Longer* (Los Angeles: Sherbourne Press, 1973), p. 129.

We are grateful to Fran Presley for her contribution on the relationship between sunglasses, sunshine and menstrual periods.

Other views linking exercise with health include P. A. Rechnitzer et al., "Effects of a 24-Week Exercise Programme on Normal Adults and Patients with Previous Myocardial Infarction," *British Medical Journal*, March 25, 1967, pp. 734–35; Lenore R. Zohman and Jerome S. Tobis, "The Effect of Exercise Training on Patients with Angina Pectoris," *Archives of Physical Medicine and Rehabilitation* 48 (October 1967), pp. 525–32; E. Maurice Heller, "Rehabilitation After Myocardial Infarction: Practical Experience with a Graded Exercise Program," *Canadian Medical Association Journal* 97 (July 1, 1967), pp. 22–27; "Exercise and Heart Disease," editorial, *Journal of the American Medical Association* (*JAMA*) 200, no. 2 (April 10, 1967), pp. 173–74; R. T. Bugg, "Mending Hearts at Home," *Today's Health*, November 1967, pp. 52–55; Ralph Bugg, "They're Mending Hearts with Exercise," *Today's Health*, October 1967, pp. 50–55; Arthur J. Snider, "Run for Your Life," *Science Digest*, May 1967, pp. 80 ff.

Kenneth H. Cooper, "Guidelines in the Management of the Exercising Patient," *JAMA*, March 9, 1970, pp. 1663–67; Peter F. Cohn et al., "Diagnostic Accuracy of Two-Step Post-exercise ECG," *JAMA*, April 24, 1972, pp. 501–6; Paul Rochmis and Henry Blackburn, "Exercise Tests: A Survey of Procedures, Safety, and Litigation Experience in Approximately 170,000 Tests," *JAMA*, August 23, 1971, pp. 1061–66; E. Cheraskin, W. M. Ringsdorf, Jr., D. W. Michael and B. S. Hicks, "The Exercise Profile," *Journal of the American Geriatrics Society*, 21, no. 5, pp. 208–15; *Physical Fitness Research Digest*, ser. 2, no. 3 (July 1972) and ser. 2, no. 4 (October 1972); Committee on Exercise and Physical Fitness, "Evaluation for Exercise Participation: The Apparently Healthy Individual," *JAMA*, February 14, 1972, pp. 900–1; "Six-Month Exercising Course Assists Postinfarct Patients," *Medical Tribune*, November 17, 1971; "Life of Labor May Prevent Heart Attack," *Family Practice News*, October 15, 1972, pp. 1, 46.

6. *How to Relax and Reduce Stress*

The mental sets and the general approach to this chapter have come from many sources and many persons. Some of the books that have contributed include Arnold A. Hutschnecker, *The Will to Live* (Englewood Cliffs, N.J.: Prentice-Hall, 1958); Carl R. Rogers, *On Becoming a Person: A Therapist's View of Psychotherapy* (Boston: Houghton Mifflin, 1961); Arthur Janov, *The Primal Scream* (New York: Putnam,

1970); Maxwell Maltz, *Psycho-Cybernetics: A New Way to Get More Living Out of Life* (Englewood Cliffs, N.J.: Prentice-Hall, 1960); Willard and Marguerite Beecher, *Beyond Success and Failure: Ways to Self-Reliance and Maturity* (New York: Julian Press, 1966); Philip Kapleau, ed., *Three Pillars of Zen* (New York: Harper & Row, 1965); Ken Keyes, Jr., *Handbook to Higher Consciousness* (Berkeley, Calif.: Living Love Center, 1973).

A good coverage of psychosomatic disorders is "Psycho-Somatic Medicine," *MD*, May 1971, pp. 121–32.

Philip Kapleau, *Wheel of Death* (New York: Harper & Row, 1971) is a valuable guide to resolving your death fears.

The quotation of Dr. Martin Luther King, Jr., is from Sandra Haggerty's column, "On Being Black," Texarkana *Gazette*, March 3, 1974.

For detailed investigation of meditation and the alpha state, see especially Charles T. Tart, ed., *Altered States of Consciousness: A Book of Readings* (New York: John Wiley & Sons, 1969), which consists of thirty-five articles by a large cross-section of writers in the field; three articles that might be mentioned are "On Meditation" by Edward W. Maupin, "Experimental Meditation" by Arthur J. Deikman and "Meditative Techniques in Psychotherapy" by Wolfgang Kretschmer.

A good roundup of research on biofeedback is Marvin Karlins and Lewis M. Andrews, *Biofeedback: Turning On the Power of Your Mind* (Philadelphia: J. B. Lippincott, 1972). A good journalistic report of alpha training can be seen in "Alpha 'Beta' for Mind Control," *Dallas Morning News*, July 22, 1973, p. 34A.

Blood pressure lowering and other benefits of alpha state were reported in Robert Keith Wallace and Herbert Benson, "The Physiology of Meditation," *Scientific American* 226, no. 2 (February 1972), pp. 84–90, and Herbert Benson et al., "Decreased Systolic Blood Pressure Through Operant Conditioning Techniques in Patients with Essential Hypertension," *Science* 173, August 20, 1971, pp. 740–42. See also Robert Keith Wallace, Herbert Benson and Archie F. Wilson, "A Wakeful Hypometabolic Physiologic State," *American Journal of Physiology* 221, no. 3 (September 1971), pp. 795–99; Marjorie Toomin, "Alpha Meditation and Transpersonal States," paper read at American Psychological Association convention, Oahu, Hawaii, 1972; and Marjorie Kawin Toomin and Hershel Toomin, "Bio-Feedback: Fact and Fantasy," paper presented to California State Psychological Association convention, Los Angeles, January 29, 1972.

The drug-controlling effects of alpha can be seen in "Meditation May Find Use in Medical Practice," *JAMA*, January 17, 1972.

The problem driver, regarding accidents, is reviewed in "What You Can Do About the Fourth Biggest Killer," *Patient Care*, October 15, 1972, pp. 102 ff.

8. *To Renew a Nation*

The conclusion in regard to heart transplants is that of the authors, although it is one readily evident to anyone who reads. As of this writing there are five patients still alive who received heart transplants more than four years previously.

For a view of the newer, more pertinent coronary operations, see John L. Ochsner and Noel L. Mills, "Present Status of Coronary Artery Surgery," *Resident and Staff Physician*, February 1974, pp. 30–38.

An Armamentarium of Healthful Reading

We do not recommend any additional reading until you are changing your life style. At first it is better to use your time doing what is necessary, rather than reading about it. Once you have a good start on the program, and have the time and the inclination to read more, we suggest the following book list.

Seven of these we would classify, for various reasons, as "priority" reading. Most, if not all, are also available in paperback.

E. Cheraskin and W. M. Ringsdorf, Jr., *New Hope for Incurable Diseases* (New York: Exposition Press, 1971).

Adelle Davis, *Let's Eat Right to Keep Fit* (New York: Harcourt Brace Jovanovich, 1970).

Kenneth H. Cooper, *The New Aerobics* (New York: M. Evans, 1970).

Roger J. Williams, *Nutrition Against Disease: Environmental Prevention* (New York: Pitman Publishing, 1971).

Catharyn Elwood, *Feel Like a Million!* (New York: Devin-Adair, 1956).

Joe D. Nichols and James Presley, *"Please, Doctor, Do Something!"* (Atlanta, Tex.: Natural Food Associates, 1972).

Kahlil Gibran, *The Prophet* (New York: Alfred A. Knopf, 1923).

If you wish to go deeper into the various subjects discussed in this book, the following titles may prove helpful. You may think of others we have inadvertently left out.

Nutrition

E. Cheraskin, W. M. Ringsdorf, Jr., and J. W. Clark, *Diet and Disease* (Emmaus, Pa.: Rodale Books, 1968).

Weston A. Price, *Nutrition and Physical Degeneration: A Comparison of Primitive and Modern Diets and Their Effects* (Santa Monica, Calif.: Price-Pottenger Foundation, 1945).

T. L. Cleave, G. D. Campbell and N. S. Painter, *Diabetes, Coronary Thrombosis, and the Saccharine Disease,* 2d ed. (Bristol, England: John Wright & Sons, 1969).

E. M. Abrahamson and A. W. Pezet, *Body, Mind, and Sugar* (New York: Holt, Rinehart & Winston, 1951; paperback, Pyramid Books, 1971).

Carlton Fredericks and Herman Goodman, *Low Blood Sugar and You* (New York: Grosset & Dunlap, 1969).

George Watson, *Nutrition and Your Mind: The Psychochemical Response* (New York: Harper & Row, 1972).

John M. Ellis and James Presley, *Vitamin B_6: The Doctor's Report* (New York: Harper & Row, 1973).

Linus Pauling, *Vitamin C and the Common Cold* (San Francisco: W. H. Freeman, 1970).

Irwin Stone, *The Healing Factor: "Vitamin C" Against Disease* (New York: Grosset & Dunlap, 1972).

Wilfred E. Shute with Harold J. Taub, *Vitamin E for Ailing and Healthy Hearts* (New York: Pyramid House, 1970).

Melvin E. Page, *Degeneration-Regeneration* (St. Petersburg Beach, Fla.: Nutritional Development, 1949).

Adelle Davis, *Let's Cook It Right* (New York: Harcourt Brace Jovanovich, 1962).

Frances Moore Lappe, *Diet for a Small Planet* (New York: Friends of the Earth/Ballantine Books, 1971).

Herbert G. Birch and Joan Dye Gussow, *Disadvantaged Children: Health, Nutrition and School Failure* (New York: Harcourt Brace Jovanovich, 1970; and Grune & Stratton, 1970).

Smoking

Herbert Brean, *How to Stop Smoking* (New York: Vanguard, 1958; paperback, Pocket Books, 1970).

Walter S. Ross, *You Can Quit Smoking in 14 Days* (New York: Reader's Digest Press, 1974).

Interpersonal Relationships

Thomas A. Harris, *I'm OK—You're OK: A Practical Guide to Transactional Analysis* (New York: Harper & Row, 1969).

Muriel James and Dorothy Jongeward, *Born to Win: Transactional Analysis with Gestalt Experiments* (Reading, Mass.: Addison-Wesley, 1971).

George R. Bach and Peter Wyden, *The Intimate Enemy* (New York: William Morrow, 1969).

On Children

Ray C. Wunderlich, *Allergy, Brains, and Children Coping* (St. Petersburg, Fla.: Johnny Reads, Inc., 1973).

Rudolf Dreikurs and Vicki Soltz, *Children: The Challenge* (New York: Duell, Sloan & Pearce, 1964).

Haim G. Ginott, *Between Parent and Child* (New York: Macmillan, 1967).

Growth Books

Arnold A. Hutschnecker, *The Will to Live* (Englewood Cliffs, N.J.: Prentice-Hall, 1958).

Carl R. Rogers, *On Becoming a Person: A Therapist's View of Psychotherapy* (Boston: Houghton Mifflin, 1961).

Arthur Janov, *The Primal Scream* (New York: Putnam, 1970).

Maxwell Maltz, *Psycho-Cybernetics: A New Way to Get More Living Out of Life* (Englewood Cliffs, N.J.: Prentice-Hall, 1960).

Willard and Marguerite Beecher, *Beyond Success and Failure: Ways to Self-Reliance and Maturity* (New York: Julian Press, 1966).

Milton Mayeroff, *On Caring* (New York: Harper & Row, 1971).

Philip Kapleau, ed., *Three Pillars of Zen* (New York: Harper & Row, 1965).

Ken Keyes, Jr., *Handbook to Higher Consciousness* (Berkeley, Calif.: Living Love Center, 1973).

William C. Schutz, *Here Comes Everybody: Body-mind and Encounter Culture* (New York: Harper & Row, 1971).

To Reduce Inner Stress

Philip Kapleau, *Wheel of Death: A Collection of Writings from Zen Buddhist and Other Sources on Dying-Death-Rebirth* (New York: Harper & Row, 1971).

Yoga

Indra Devi, *Yoga for Americans* (Englewood Cliffs, N.J.: Prentice-Hall, 1959).

Charlotte Rudeau, *Josie, Jay, Jerri and Yoga* (Nassau, Bahamas: Paradise Island Yoga Retreat, 1973). Also *Symphony in Yoga* (1971).

Swami Vishnu Devananda, *The Complete Illustrated Book of Yoga* (Nassau, Bahamas: Paradise Island Yoga Retreat).

Social Trends

Erich Fromm, *The Revolution of Hope* (New York: Harper & Row, 1968).

Alvin Toffler, *Future Shock* (New York: Random House, 1970).

Charles A. Reich, *The Greening of America: How the Youth Revolution Is Trying to Make America Liveable* (New York: Random House, 1970).

Sidney Jourard, *The Transparent Self* (Princeton, N.J.: D. Van Nostrand, 1964).

Frederick S. Perls, *Gestalt Therapy Verbatim* (Lafayette, Calif.: Real People Press, 1969).

Ecology

G. Tyler Miller, Jr., *Replenish the Earth: A Primer in Human Ecology* (Belmont, Calif.: Wadsworth Publishing, 1972).

Donella H. Meadows, Dennis L. Meadows, Jorgen Randers and William W. Behrens III, *The Limits to Growth: A Report for the Club of Rome's Project on the Predicament of Mankind* (New York: Universe Books, 1972; paperback, New American Library).

Rachel Carson, *Silent Spring* (Boston: Houghton Mifflin, 1962).

General

William Proxmire, *You Can Do It! Senator Proxmire's Exercise, Diet and Relaxation Plan* (New York: Simon & Schuster, 1973).

Earl Ubell, *How to Save Your Life* (New York: Harcourt Brace Jovanovich, 1973).

Magazines

Prevention, Rodale Press, Emmaus, Pa. 18049 (all issues).